Grade 2

Your Turn

Practice Book

www.mheonline.com/readingwonders

Send all inquiries to:
McGraw-Hill Education
Two Penn Plaza
New York, NY 10121

Printed in the United States of America.

7 8 9 LHS 21 20 19 18 B

Contents

Unit 1 • Friends and Family

Week 1

Friends Help Friends

Week 2

Families Around the World

Week 3

Pets Are Our Friends

Week 4

Animals Need Care

Week 5

Families Working Together

Contents

Unit 2 • Animal Discoveries

Week 1

Animals and Nature

Week 2

Animals in Stories

Week 3

Animal Habitats

Week 4

Baby Animals

Week 5

Animals in Poems

Unit 3 • Live and Learn

Week 1

The Earth's Forces

Week 2

Look at the Sky

Week 3

Ways People Help

Week 4

Weather Alert!

Week 5

Express Yourself

Contents

Unit 4 • Our Life/Our World

Contents

Unit 5 • Let's Make a Difference

Contents

Unit 6 • How on Earth?

Week 1

Plant Myths and Facts

Week 2

We Need Energy

Week 3

Team Up to Explore

Week 4

Money Matters

Week 5

The World of Ideas

Name ______________________________

actions	afraid	depend	nervously
peered	perfectly	rescue	secret

Use what you know about the words in the sentences to choose the word that makes sense in each blank. Then write the word on the line.

1. The boy can ______________ on his friend to help him.
2. She ______________ into the dark room.
3. The man helped ______________ people from danger.
4. The friends sang the song together ______________ in tune.
5. The girl was not ______________ to try something new.
6. Do not tell anyone the ______________.
7. The mouse looked around ______________ for the cat.
8. We watched the soccer players' quick ______________.

Name ______________________________

Listen to each short vowel sound as you say the words *pan* and *fit*.

A. Say the name of each picture. Circle the word that has the same vowel sound as the picture name. Write the word on the line.

1. six fun ______________

2. lot wag ______________

The endings *-s* or *-es* make nouns mean more than one.

B. Read each word. Write the base word.

3. mats ______________ **4.** bags ______________

5. kisses ______________ **6.** fans ______________

Name ______________________________

Read the passage. Use the visualize strategy to picture in your mind what is happening in the story.

A Bicycle Built for Two

It was a beautiful fall day. The sun was shining. The
11 leaves were red and gold and orange. Squirrel wanted to
21 go for a bike ride, but his bike was broken.

31 "I can't fix this by myself," thought Squirrel. "I will
41 need some help."

44 Squirrel went to see Fox. "Will you help me fix my
55 bike?" Squirrel asked.

58 "I'd like to help, but I am too busy cooking soup,"
69 said Fox.

71 So Squirrel continued on. He saw Bear and asked
80 for help.

82 "I'm too busy right now washing clothes. Maybe I can
92 help next week," Bear said.

Name ______________________________

97 Squirrel shook his head. He wanted to fix his bike
107 and take a ride today. Just then, Rabbit came along and
118 asked Squirrel why he looked so sad. Squirrel explained
127 the problem. "You are probably too busy to help me,"
137 sighed Squirrel.

139 Rabbit looked over the bike. He turned a wire
148 here. He oiled a wheel there. "Now let's give it a try,"
160 Rabbit said.

162 The two friends climbed on the bike. They rode
171 for a long time through the woods, enjoying the
180 beautiful day.

Name ______________________________

A. Reread the passage and answer the questions.

1. Why was Fox too busy to help Squirrel fix his bike?

____

____

2. Why was Bear too busy to help Squirrel fix his bike?

____

____

3. Why were Squirrel and Rabbit both able to ride the bike?

____

____

B. Work with a partner. Read the passage aloud. Pay attention to how you use your voice to show feelings. Stop after one minute. Fill out the chart.

	Words Read	–	Number of Errors	=	Words Correct Score
First Read		–		=	
Second Read		–		=	

Name ____

Read the selection. Complete the Key Details chart.

Detail	Detail	Detail

Name ______________________________

Thanks, Friend!

"Planting a garden is hard work," says Mouse. "It takes me a long time to dig each hole." "I can help!" says Mole. Mole digs the holes quickly. Mouse plants the seeds.

Answer the questions about the text.

1. How do you know this text is fantasy?

____

____

2. Why is it easy for Mole to dig the holes?

____

3. Why does Mole dig so many holes?

____

____

Name ______________________________

To figure out new words, look at word parts. A root word may have the ending ***-s, -es, -ed,*** or ***-ing***. The endings *-s, -es,* and *-ing* mean the action is happening now. The ending *-ed* means the action happened in the past.

Write the meaning of each underlined word. Circle whether the action is happening now or in the past.

1. "Will you help me fix my bike?" Squirrel asked.

   Meaning: ______________________________

   now past

2. "I'd like to help, but I am too busy cooking soup," said Fox.

   Meaning: ______________________________

   now past

3. "I'm too busy right now washing clothes."

   Meaning: ______________________________

   now past

4. Squirrel explained the problem.

   Meaning: ______________________________

   now past

5. Rabbit looked over the bike.

   Meaning: ______________________________

   now past

Name ______________________

A. Read the draft model. Use the questions that follow the draft to help you add details that describe the event.

Draft Model

Ronnie and Kevin went on a picnic. When the friends got there, they set out all the food on a blanket. Then it started to rain. The two friends quickly put everything back into the basket. They went home.

1. Where did the two friends go on their picnic?

2. What did they pack for their picnic?

3. How did the friends get home?

B. Now revise the draft by adding details that clearly describe what happened at the picnic.

____

____

____

____

____

____

Name ____

Anita used text evidence to answer the prompt: *Write a short poem about Mouse and Snake's friendship.*

Friends

Gossip from Skunk
made me doubt my friend Snake.
But all of my doubts
only hurt me as I nervously peeped around
looking for Snake, I fell into a hole.
I got stuck.
I couldn't climb out.
And in the end,
all I had was my friend
Who helped me, and he wasn't upset
even though I didn't trust him.

Reread the passage. Follow the directions below.

1. **Circle** the event that was important to Mouse and Snake's friendship.

2. **Draw a box** around a supporting detail that tells why Mouse was sorry.

3. **Underline** a descriptive detail that describes how Mouse felt.

4. **Write** a complete sentence from Anita's poem.

____.

Name ______________________________

aside	culture	fair	invited
language	plead	scurries	share

A. Read each clue below. Then find the vocabulary word on the right that matches the clue. Draw a line from the clue to the word.

1. was asked to come somewhere	**a.** language
2. give part of something	**b.** plead
3. the words people speak	**c.** fair
4. runs quickly	**d.** invited
5. moved to one side	**e.** share
6. a way of life	**f.** culture
7. beg	**g.** aside
8. honest	**h.** scurries

B. Choose one vocabulary word from the box above. Write the word in a sentence of your own.

9. ______________________________

____

Name ____

Listen to each short vowel sound as you say the words ***bed, top***, and ***sun***.

A. Write the words in the box in the correct list below.

went	job	tub	tell	not	hut

1. What words have the short *e* sound, as in ***bed***?

_______________ _______________

2. What words have the short *o* sound, as in ***top***?

_______________ _______________

3. What words have the short *u* sound, as in ***sun***?

_______________ _______________

The endings ***-s*** or ***-es*** can be added to a verb to show action that is taking place now.

B. Add *-s* or *-es* to the end of each word. Write the new word.

4. pass _______________ 5. yell _______________

6. tag _______________ 7. mix _______________

Name ______________________________

Read the passage. Use the visualize strategy to picture in your mind what is happening in the story.

The Food Festival

Van and his family went to the local food festival.
10 Van's eyes opened wide. He was amazed at how this
20 quiet street had been changed. On each side, food
29 booths were set up showing colorful flags. He knew
38 a few. There was Mexico and there was China. Van
48 followed his mom, dad, and sister down the street.

57 Mom stopped at the first booth. People were selling
66 Greek salad there. Van's family shared a big plate of
76 salad.

77 Then they walked to the Chinese booth. They had the
87 beef noodle soup.

Name ____

90 The next stop was the Indian booth for spicy curry.
100 At the Mexican booth, they all had tamales.

108 At last, the family reached the end of the street.
118 Everyone was full. "Which food did you like the best?"
128 asked Dad.

130 The family members all spoke at once.
137 "The curry," said Van.
141 "The tamales," said his sister.
146 "The beef noodle soup," Mom said.
152 "And I liked the Greek salad best," said Dad with a
163 smile. "I guess we can agree that *all* the food here is
175 delicious."

Name ______________________________

A. Reread the passage and answer the questions.

1. Who were the characters in the story?

____

____

2. Where did the story take place?

____

____

3. What event took place at the beginning of the story?

____

____

B. Work with a partner. Read the passage aloud. Pay attention to how you use your voice to show feelings. Stop after one minute. Fill out the chart.

	Words Read	–	Number of Errors	=	Words Correct Score
First Read		–		=	
Second Read		–		=	

Name ____________________

Read the selection. Complete the Character, Setting, Events chart.

Character	Setting	Events

Name ______________________________

Two Kinds of Football

Tim and Victor agreed to play football with their families. Tim said, "I brought a football." Victor said, "I brought a soccer ball. Soccer is called football in many countries." They learned to play two kinds of football.

Answer the questions about the text.

1. How do you know this text is realistic fiction?

____

____

2. What happens at the beginning of the story?

____

3. What happens in the middle?

____

4. What happens at the end?

____

Name ______________________________

To figure out a new word, separate the **root word** from the ending. The endings *-s, -es,* and *-ing* mean the action is happening now. The ending *-ed* means the action happened in the past.

A. Read each sentence. Look at each underlined word. Draw a line between the root word and the ending.

1. Van's eyes opened wide.

2. Food booths were set up showing colorful flags.

3. People were selling Greek salad there.

B. Underline the verb in each sentence. Then change each verb so that it tells about action happening now. Write the new word.

4. Mom stopped at the first booth.

____

5. At last, the family reached the end of the street.

____

Name ______________________________

A. Read the draft model. Use the questions that follow the draft to help you write a strong beginning for the story.

Draft Model

She went to the store to get some milk. It was a long walk. When she got there she was upset. She forgot her money. The store owner was very kind. He said she could take the milk and bring the money later.

1. Who is the character in the story?

2. Where does the story take place?

3. What information will make readers want to continue reading?

B. Now revise the draft by adding a strong beginning that grabs the reader's attention and tells the character and setting.

____

____

____

____

____

____

Name ____

Alex used text evidence to answer the prompt: *Write a paragraph that describes a meal that Rubina's family shares with friends.*

On Saturday, we invited our friends, the Garcias, to share a meal with us. Ami wanted to serve foods from our culture. However, I begged and she agreed to serve an American meal. I searched for recipes, and Ami and I talked about what we should serve. We decided on pizza topped with vegetables, a big salad, and ice cream. Sana and I helped to set the table. We used a red cloth with blue napkins. With our white plates, the table looked like an American flag! Mrs. Garcia brought us fresh strawberries from the market. Maryam ate two slices of pizza and two servings of salad. The sauce was all over her face! Sana was a little mad because Maryam took the last slice of pizza. She was happier, though, when Ami served her a big bowl of strawberries!

Reread the passage. Follow the directions below.

1. **Circle** the event that Alex uses at the beginning of his model.
2. **Draw a box** around the words that describe the meal.
3. **Underline** a detail that tells how Sana acted during the meal.
4. **Write** an exclamation that Alex included in his response.

____.

Name ________________________________

decide	different	friendship	glance
proper	relationship	stares	trade

A. Read each clue below. Then find the vocabulary word on the right that matches the clue. Draw a line from the clue to the word.

1. look at quickly — **a.** proper

2. not the same — **b.** friendship

3. correct — **c.** decide

4. looks at for a long time — **d.** trade

5. make up your mind — **e.** glance

6. being pals — **f.** different

7. give one thing for another — **g.** relationship

8. a connection with someone — **h.** stares

B. Choose one vocabulary word from the box above. Write the word in a sentence of your own.

9. ________________________________

____

Name ____

Two letters can be blended together, such as ***cl, dr, sk, sl,*** and ***st.*** Listen to the beginning sounds in ***slip*** and the ending sounds in ***best.***

A. Look at the picture. Write the missing blend for each word.

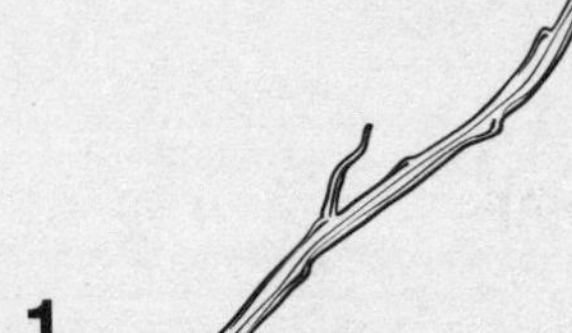

1. __________ ick

2. ma __________

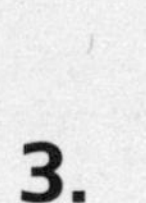

3. __________ ock

4. __________ ed

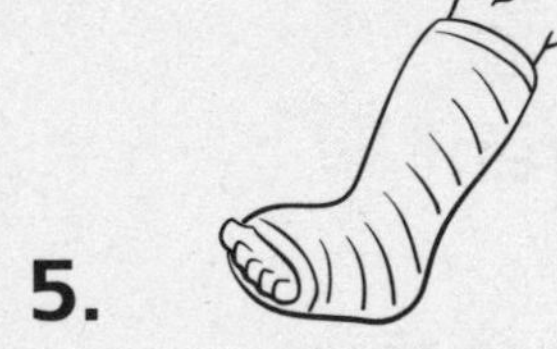

5. ca __________

6. __________ ess

When two consonants come between two vowels, you divide the word between the two consonants to find the syllables.

B. Divide each word into syllables. Write the syllables on the lines provided.

7. velvet __________ __________

8. contest __________ __________

9. picnic __________ __________

10. sudden __________ __________

Name ______________________________

Read the passage. Ask and answer questions as you read to check your understanding.

A Pet of His Own

Jeff lived with his family and their three pets. His
10 sister Kim had a bird. His brother Rick had two mice.
21 Jeff wanted a pet of his own. "May I get a snake?" he
34 asked his parents. He was polite because he knew good
44 manners were important.

47 "A snake will eat my bird," shrieked Kim loudly. Her
57 yell upset her bird. The bird started to chirp.

66 Jeff had another idea. "May I get a cat?" he asked
77 politely.

78 "A cat will eat my bird," cried Kim.

86 "And a cat will eat my mice," said Rick.

Name ______________________________

95 Jeff was stumped by his pet problem and didn't know
105 how to solve it. He wanted a pet that was different and
117 unique. There was already one bird and two mice. He
127 couldn't get a snake or a cat. What kind of pet wouldn't
139 disturb or upset the others?

144 Then one day Jeff saw an ad for a rabbit. This pet was
157 different. This pet could get along with the others.

166 Jeff's parents got him the rabbit. He was so thrilled to
177 have a pet of his own that he shouted for joy.

Name ______________________________

A. Reread the passage and answer the questions.

1. Who were the characters in the story?

____

____

2. Where did the story take place?

____

____

3. What event took place at the end of the story?

____

____

B. Work with a partner. Read the passage aloud. Pay attention to how your voice rises and falls as you speak naturally. Stop after one minute. Fill out the chart.

	Words Read	–	Number of Errors	=	Words Correct Score
First Read		–		=	
Second Read		–		=	

Name ______________________________

Read the selection. Complete the Character, Setting, Events chart.

Character	Setting	Events

Name ______________________________

The Perfect Reading Partner

Reading was not easy for Lizzie. One day, her cat Gumbo jumped in her lap while she was reading. Lizzie read aloud to Gumbo. She did not make one mistake. Gumbo was a great listener!

Answer the questions about the text.

1. How can you tell that this text is fiction?

____

____

2. What happens at the beginning of the story?

____

3. What happens in the middle?

____

4. What happens at the end?

____

Name ______________________________

Look at this example of **context clues**. The underlined words explain what *polite* means.

He was **polite** because he knew <u>good manners were important</u>.

Read each sentence. Then circle the meaning of the word in bold print that makes sense. Underline the context clues.

1. "A snake will eat my bird," **shrieked** Kim loudly.

   yelled　　　　whispered

2. Jeff was **stumped** by his pet problem and didn't know how to solve it.

   happy　　　　confused

3. He wanted a pet that was different and **unique**.

   the same　　　　not like others

4. What kind of pet wouldn't **disturb** or upset the others?

   bother　　　　enjoy

5. He was so **thrilled** to have a pet of his own that he shouted for joy.

   angry　　　　excited

Name ______________________________

A. Read the draft model. Use the questions that follow the draft to help you use more precise words.

Draft Model

My kitten is a good size for my family's small apartment. She can sleep on my lap. She has nice fur. My kitten likes to be outside and so do I.

1. What size is the kitten?

2. What color is the kitten's fur? How does it feel?

3. What does the kitten like to do outside?

B. Now revise the draft by replacing general words with more precise, interesting words about the kitten.

____

____

____

____

____

____

____

Name ____________________

James used text evidence to answer the prompt: *Add an event to the end of the story in which the boy gets a puppy.*

I finally got a puppy! Mom and Dad told me I had taken good care of Norman, so they thought I could take care of a puppy! We went to an animal shelter where there were lots of animals. I chose a little puppy with floppy ears. He is mostly white with patches of black and brown. I call my puppy Patches.

At first, Patches and Norman didn't get along. I think Norman was jealous. He would swim around his bowl and just look at Patches. Then one day, I left Norman on the table in the sun. Patches pulled at my sleeve until I moved Norman. Now Norman and Patches are best friends! I miss them both when I'm at school. When I get home, we all go to the park!

Reread the passage. Follow the directions below.

1. **Circle** the event that James uses to begin his answer.

2. **Draw a box** around the precise words that James uses to describe his puppy.

3. **Underline** a descriptive detail that shows the boy's feelings about his pets.

4. **Write** the subject of this sentence: I call my puppy Patches.

____________________.

Name ______________________________

allowed	care	excited	needs
roam	safe	wandered	wild

Choose the word that makes sense in each blank. Then write the word on the line.

1. An animal living in the ______________ is different than a pet.

2. Dogs are not ______________ in the park.

3. A cat that has ______________ from its yard might get lost.

4. The girl takes good ______________ of her pet hamster.

5. The children were ______________ about getting a new pet.

6. A pet's ______________ include water, food, and exercise.

7. Our cat keeps her kittens ______________ from danger.

8. Pets live with people, but animals in the jungle ______________ free.

Name ______________________________

The letter ***a*** can stand for the short ***a*** sound you hear in ***can***. The long ***a*** sound you hear in ***cane*** can be spelled ***a_e***.

A. Circle one short *a* word and one long *a* word in each sentence. Write each word in the correct list below.

1. The ducks swam in the lake.

2. We wave to the man on the bus.

short *a*	**long *a***
3. ______________	**5.** ______________
4. ______________	**6.** ______________

The ending ***-ing*** can be added to a verb to show that an action is happening right now. The ending ***-ed*** can be added to a verb to show action that has already happened.

B. Add *-ed* and *-ing* to the end of each word. Write the two new words.

7. fix ______________ ______________

8. pack ______________ ______________

9. play ______________ ______________

10. lock ______________ ______________

Name ____________________

Read the passage. Ask and answer questions as you read to check your understanding.

A Fire Dog

Wilshire is a fire dog. He lives in the city. When
11 Wilshire first came to the fire station, he was just three
22 months old. He lived at the fire station day and night.
33 Fifty firefighters lived and worked there, too. They took
42 care of Wilshire. They fed the young dog. They gave
52 him water to drink.

56 The firefighters hired a dog trainer. The trainer gave
65 Wilshire lessons. He helped Wilshire learn to live in the
75 fire station. He showed Wilshire where he could go. He
85 showed Wilshire where he was not allowed to go.

94 Then it was time for exercise. Wilshire didn't even
103 have to go outside. He was trained to run on a treadmill
115 inside the station.

Name ____________________

Fire dogs like Wilshire are often a breed called Dalmatians.

118 Soon Wilshire became close pals with one firefighter.
126 Now Wilshire and the firefighter spend a shift at the
136 fire station together. Then the firefighter takes Wilshire
144 home. This gives Wilshire a break from the busy station.
154 He also has fun meeting and playing with other dogs.

164 Wilshire got even more training. Now he can do fire
174 safety tricks. He visits schools and shows children how
183 to "Stop, Drop, and Roll." All that work keeps Wilshire
193 very busy!

Name ______________________________

A. Reread the passage and answer the questions.

1. How did the firefighters take care of Wilshire?

____

____

2. Why did the firefighter take Wilshire home?

____

____

3. What does a Dalmatian look like?

____

____

B. Work with a partner. Read the passage aloud. Pay attention to how your voice rises and falls as you speak naturally. Stop after one minute. Fill out the chart.

	Words Read	–	Number of Errors	=	Words Correct Score
First Read		–		=	
Second Read		–		=	

Name ______________________________

Read the selection. Complete the Key Details chart.

Detail	Detail	Detail

Name ____

The Foster Pet

Amy's family has a foster pet. They feed and play with Rocky and take him to the vet. They train him to follow commands. When Rocky gets bigger, another family will give him a lasting home.

Amy trains Rocky to walk on a leash.

Answer the questions about the selection.

1. How can you tell this text is a nonfiction narrative?

____

____

2. What is one way that Amy trains Rocky? How did you find this information?

____

____

3. What does the text help you learn about a foster pet?

____

____

Name ____________________

To figure out a new word, separate the **root word** from the ending. The endings *-s, -es,* and *-ing* mean the action is happening now. The ending *-ed* means the action happened in the past.

Read each sentence. Look at each underlined word. Draw a line between the root word and the ending. Then write the meaning of the word.

1. He lives in the city.

____

2. Fifty firefighters lived and worked there, too.

____

3. He helped Wilshire learn to live in the fire station.

____

4. Then the firefighter takes Wilshire home.

____

5. He also has fun meeting and playing with other dogs.

____

Name ____

A. Read the draft model. Use the questions that follow the draft to help you think about how to use sequence words.

Draft Model

Here's how to give a dog a bath. Fill the tub with warm water. Get the dog in the tub and wash her with soap. Rinse her with plenty of fresh water. Dry the dog with a towel.

1. To give a dog a bath, what do you do first?

2. What do you do next? Then what?

3. What is the last thing you do?

B. Now revise the draft by adding sequence words such as *first, next, then,* and *last* to help readers understand the order of ideas.

____

____

____

____

____

____

Name ____

Sophie used text evidence to answer the prompt: ***In your opinion, is it easier to care for a baby rhino or a dog?***

In my opinion, it would be easier to care for a dog than a baby rhino. I can see on page 86 that rhinos are large animals. They need plenty of space to play. There is a park near my house, but a rhino would need more room. I also read on page 89 that Lola drank more than a gallon of milk five times a day! I think that would be a lot of work.

Caring for a dog would be much easier. I know that dogs need food and water. I could do that before I go to school. When I got home from school, I could walk a dog in the park. After that, I could brush a dog. Then I would feed a dog its dinner. I think caring for a dog would be much more fun and easier than caring for a rhino.

Reread the passage. Follow the directions below.

1. **Draw a box** around the sentence in which Sophie introduces the topic and states her opinion.

2. **Underline** the sentences that tell the sequence, or order, in which Sophie would care for a dog each day.

3. **Circle** a linking word that shows Sophie's opinion about caring for a dog and a rhino.

4. **Write** a predicate from any sentence in Sophie's model.

____.

Name ______________________________

checks	choose	chores	cost
customers	jobs	spend	tools

A. Choose the word that makes sense for each clue. Write the word on the line.

1. pay money to buy something ____________

2. looks at something closely to make sure it is okay ____________

3. people who buy things ____________

4. equipment used to make or fix things ____________

5. small jobs around the house ____________

6. how much you have to pay for something ____________

7. work people do to earn money ____________

8. to decide on one thing rather than another ____________

B. Choose one vocabulary word from the box above. Write the word in a sentence of your own.

9. ______________________________

____

Name ____

The letter ***i*** can stand for the short ***i*** sound you hear in ***fit***. The long ***i*** sound you hear in ***fine*** can be spelled ***i_e***.

A. Read each word. Circle the words with the short *i* sound. Underline the words with the long *i* sound.

pipe did tip five hike fin side pick

A possessive noun ends with an apostrophe (') and an ***s*** to show who owns something.

B. Rewrite each phrase using a possessive noun.

1. the kite that belongs to the girl

____

2. the job that belongs to Mom

____

3. the dish that belongs to the cat

____

4. the ball that belongs to the dog

____

Name ______________________________

Read the passage. Ask and answer questions as you read to check your understanding.

Family Business

Families may start up a business. The family
08 members all pitch in to make it work. Then the business
19 is passed down through the family. Here's one family
28 business that has been around for 95 years.

36 In 1916, two families started a new business. They
45 opened a coffee company. They roasted the coffee beans
54 by hand. There were no cars then. They used horses and
65 wagons to deliver the coffee.

70 The coffee business grew. More family members came
78 to work for the company. In 1918, the company was able
89 to buy its first truck.

Name ____________________

Family Business Then and Now

1916	Today
Roasted coffee beans by hand. Delivered coffee using a horse and wagon.	Sell coffee in stores, restaurants, and online. Make ads for TV.

94 In the 1940s, sons of the owners joined the business.
104 The company grew. It sold coffee to restaurants. The
113 company soon needed a bigger office.

119 By the 1990s, the third generation was working for the
129 company. The company started selling its coffee in new
138 places. They sold coffee food stores. They made ads for
148 TV. In 2007, they opened an online store.

156 These family members worked hard. They made their
164 business a success. Now they can pass it on to the next
176 generation.

Name ____

A. Reread the passage and answer the questions.

1. What happened in 1916?

____

____

2. What happened in the 1940s?

____

____

3. What happened in 2007?

____

____

B. Work with a partner. Read the passage aloud. Pay attention to how you pause and group words together. Stop after one minute. Fill out the chart.

	Words Read	–	Number of Errors	=	Words Correct Score
First Read		–		=	
Second Read		–		=	

Name ______________________________

Read the selection. Complete the Key Details chart.

Detail	**Detail**	**Detail**

Name ____

Family Pizza Shop

Some families own a pizza shop. Everyone helps out. The adults make the food and help customers. The kids can help clean tables and windows after school.

Adults' Jobs	Kids' Jobs
make food	clean tables
help customers	clean windows

Answer the questions about the text.

1. How can you tell this is an informational text?

____

____

2. What does the chart show?

____

____

3. What are the adults' jobs in a pizza shop?

____

____

Name ____

To figure out new words, look at word parts. A root word may have the ending *-s, -es,* or *-ed*. The endings *-s* and *-es* mean a noun is plural. The ending *-ed* means an action happened in the past.

Read each sentence. Circle the ending of the underlined word. Use what you know about root words and endings to write the meaning of each underlined word.

1. Families may start up a business.

   ____

2. Here's one family business that has been around for 95 years.

   ____

3. In 1916, two families started a new business.

   ____

4. In the 1940s, sons of the owners joined the business.

   ____

5. It sold coffee to restaurants.

   ____

Name ______________________________

A. Read the draft model. Use the questions that follow the draft to help you think about using sentences of different types and lengths.

Draft Model

I like to help my family get chores done. It makes our house clean. It also gives us free time together. That's what I love best.

1. Where could you add a question?

2. Where could you add an exclamation?

3. Which sentences could you make longer? Which sentences could you make shorter?

B. Now revise the draft by writing some questions or exclamations and by writing some long sentences and some short sentences.

____

____

____

____

____

Name ______________________________

Lee used text evidence to answer the prompt: *How are* Families Working Together *and "Why We Work" similar?*

The Gelders make goods and provide a service. I read on page 105 that they grow fruits and vegetables. On page 106, I read that they plant strawberries and they make jam with the extra berries. I can also see that they grow apples. These clues tell me that the Gelders produce food and things made from food. These are goods like the baked goods I see on page 108.

In "Why We Work," I learned that services are actions that people do. On page 109, I read that teachers provide a service. They help students learn. The Gelders also provide a service. On page 105, I read that they sell fruits and vegetables. I can see in the photo on page 107 that they sell honey and jam.

The Gelders make goods and provide services by selling their goods.

Reread the passage. Follow the directions below.

1. **Circle** two sentences that show how Lee varies his writing.

2. **Underline** text evidence that supports Lee's response to the prompt.

3. How does Lee sum up his response? **Draw a box** around his conclusion.

4. **Write** an example that shows expanding a sentence by combining ideas.

____.

Name ______________________________

adapt	climate	eager	freedom
fresh	sense	shadows	silence

Use what you know about the words in the sentences to choose the word that makes sense in each blank. Then write the word on the line.

1. My sister is excited and ______________ to learn about polar bears.
2. The quiet ______________ ended when birds began to chirp.
3. Desert animals must ______________ to hot, dry weather.
4. The air feels cool in the dark ______________ under the trees.
5. The eagle has the ______________ to fly where it wants.
6. A rainforest has a warm, wet ______________.
7. The air outside felt ______________ and clean.
8. A wild animal will run away if it feels a ______________ of danger.

Name ______________________________

The letter ***o*** can stand for the short ***o*** sound you hear in ***not***. The long ***o*** sound you hear in ***note*** can be spelled ***o_e***.

A. Read each word. Circle the words with the short *o* sound. Underline the words with the long *o* sound.

box nose rope lock pot cone dog home

Before adding ***-ed*** or ***-ing*** to some verbs with short vowels, double the final consonant. Before adding ***-ed*** or ***-ing*** to some verbs with long vowels ending in *e*, drop the final *e*.

B. Add *-ed* and *-ing* to the end of each verb. Write the two new words.

1. save ______________ ______________
2. trip ______________ ______________
3. hug ______________ ______________
4. joke ______________ ______________

Name ______________________________

Read the passage. Use the make predictions strategy to predict what will happen in the story.

Looking for Animals

Ms. Lee takes her class to the woods for a hike. She
12 tells her students to look for woodland animals. All the
22 children carry notebooks. They plan to sketch and take
31 notes about the animals they will see.

38 The group sets off down the path. High above, birds
48 sing in the trees. One boy points to what he thinks is a
61 robin. The others disagree. They say it is just a leaf.

72 The children hear hooting. It is unlike the other
81 sounds. They look up but are unable to see anything.
91 An owl looks down at them. Its brown feathers blend in
102 with the leaves. The children can not see the owl.

Name ______________________________

112 The children pass by a small pond. A deer is drinking
123 there, but it stands still as the group walks by. Its brown
135 coat makes it seem to disappear into the woods. The
145 deer slips away unseen.

149 One girl looks down at the uneven path. She sees
159 what look like small lumps of dirt. Then she stops
169 watching. The lumps jump away. No one has seen the
179 tiny toads that blend in with the ground.

187 The hike is over. The class retraces their steps back to
198 the bus. The driver unlocks the door. Maybe the class
208 can return another day to look for more animals!

Name ______________________________

A. Reread the passage and answer the questions.

1. What happened at the beginning of the story?

____

____

2. What happened in the middle of the story?

____

____

3. What happened at the end of the story?

____

____

B. Work with a partner. Read the passage aloud. Pay attention to where you pause as you read. Stop after one minute. Fill out the chart.

	Words Read	–	Number of Errors	=	Words Correct Score
First Read		–		=	
Second Read		–		=	

Name ____

Read the selection. Complete the Plot chart.

Beginning

↓

Middle

↓

End

Name ____________________

Surviving the Winter

In the summer, Jerry saw a family of chipmunks in his yard. What would they do in the cold winter? Jerry looked up chipmunk habits and learned they would hibernate all winter.

Answer the questions about the text.

1. How do you know this text is realistic fiction?

____

____

2. How does Jerry find out information about chipmunk habits?

____

3. How does Jerry know the chipmunks will survive the cold winter?

____

____

Name ______________________________

To figure out a new word, look for a **prefix**, or word part at the beginning of the word.

The prefix ***re-*** means "again."

The prefix ***un-*** means "not."

The prefix ***dis-*** means "opposite of."

Read each sentence. Underline the word that has a prefix. Then write the word and its meaning.

1. The others disagree.

____

2. They look up but are unable to see anything.

____

3. Its brown coat makes it seem to disappear into the woods.

____

4. The deer slips away unseen.

____

5. The class retraces their steps back to the bus.

____

Name ______________________________

A. Read the draft model. Use the questions that follow the draft to help you add descriptive details.

Draft Model

Meg and Tom go to the beach. They swim in the water. Meg sees birds flying in the sky. Tom finds shells on the beach. Then they see a crab near the water!

1. What kind of beach is this? What kind of day is it?

2. What details can tell more about the birds, shells, and crab that Meg and Tom see?

3. What details might tell how Meg and Tom feel about their day at the beach?

B. Now revise the draft by adding descriptive details that help readers learn more about the setting and characters.

____

____

____

____

____

Name ____

Olivia used text evidence to support the prompt: *Pretend you are the girl in* Sled Dogs Run*. You are telling your mother what you learned about fennec foxes in school.*

Today in school I learned about an animal that is very different from my sledding dogs. They are called *Fennec foxes*. I had so many questions about Fennec foxes. I wondered if they were anything like my dogs.

First, I found out that they live in the desert. They never have to get used to snow like my huskies. They also don't get the fun of running to pull a sled. Fennec foxes look similar to small dogs. They have thick fur to protect them from heat. Their special ears keep sand out.

Both animals use their tails to cover their faces when they sleep. Both animals also have special body parts that help them survive in difficult places.

Reread the passage. Follow the directions below.

1. **Draw a box** around an event that tells the girl's feelings for her sled dogs.
2. **Underline** a sentence that tells how Fennec foxes and Siberian huskies are alike.
3. **Circle** a detail that tells how Fennec foxes are different.
4. **Write** a noun that Olivia used in the first sentence.

____.

Name ______________________________

believe	delicious	feast	fond
lessons	remarkable	snatch	stories

Read the story. Choose words from the box to complete the sentences. Then write the answers on the lines.

There are some ______________ that teach ______________. This is one of those tales. Lion was very ______________ of cherries. He said, "I ______________ that cherries are the best food!"

When Lion heard that Hippo had lots of ______________ food, he went over to take a look. Seeing all of Hippos's food made him want to ______________. On the table was a bowl of the biggest cherries he had ever seen. "That's ______________!" thought Lion. He made a plan to ______________ the cherries. Then he ran home with them. At home, Lion bit into a cherry. They were wax! The cherries had not been worth taking after all.

Name ______________________________

The letter ***u*** can stand for the short ***u*** sound you hear in ***cut***. The long ***u*** sound you hear in ***cute*** can be spelled ***u_e***.

A. Choose the word from the box that names each picture. Write it on the line.

mule	tub	cub	cube

1. __________

2. __________

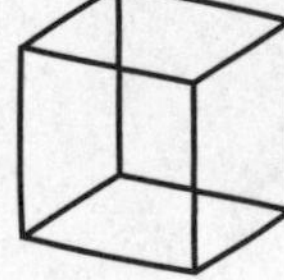

3. __________

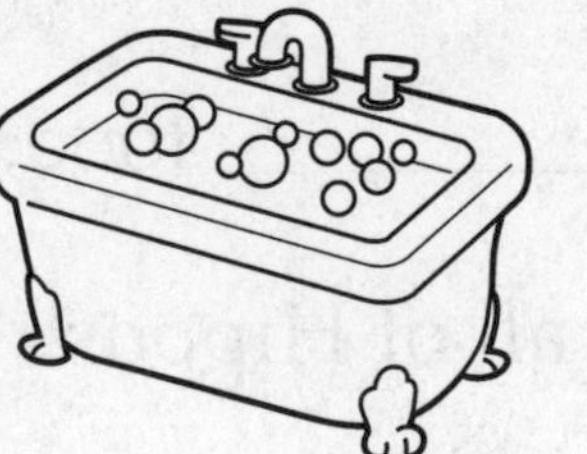

4. __________

Vowel consonant *e* syllables often have the long sound of the vowel.

B. Divide each word into syllables. Write each syllable.

5. pancake __________ __________

6. excuse __________ __________

Name ______________________________

Read the passage. Use the make predictions strategy to predict what will happen in the story.

Fox Gets Help

One day, Fox was walking in the woods. High in a
11 tree, he saw a nice bunch of grapes. "Those will make a
23 healthful snack," Fox thought. He jumped up to get the
33 grapes.

34 Fox nearly reached the grapes, but he could not jump
44 high enough. He really wanted those grapes. So Fox
53 made a plan. He got a ladder and leaned it on the tree.
66 He should be able to reach the grapes easily.

Name ____

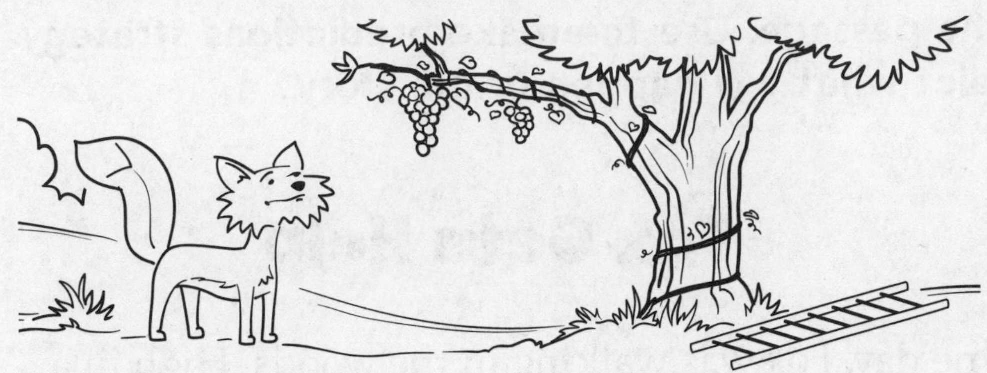

75 The wind began blowing strongly. As Fox stepped up
84 to the ladder, the wind blew it down on the ground. This
96 happened over and over again. Fox sighed loudly. He
105 was about to give up. Then Turtle crept up slowly.

115 Turtle had an idea that was helpful. He would hold
125 the ladder tightly while Fox climbed up. Fox went up the
136 ladder and picked the bunch of grapes.

143 When Fox was safely back on the ground, he shared
153 the grapes with Turtle. Fox was thankful for his friend's
163 help. Sometimes it takes a friend to help you reach a
174 goal.

Name ____

A. Reread the passage and answer the questions.

1. What was the problem in the story?

____

____

2. What steps did Fox take to solve the problem?

____

____

3. What was Fox's solution to the problem?

____

____

B. Work with a partner. Read the passage aloud. Pay attention to expression. Stop after one minute. Fill out the chart.

	Words Read	–	Number of Errors	=	Words Correct Score
First Read		–		=	
Second Read		–		=	

Name ______________________________

Read the selection. Complete the Problem and Solution chart.

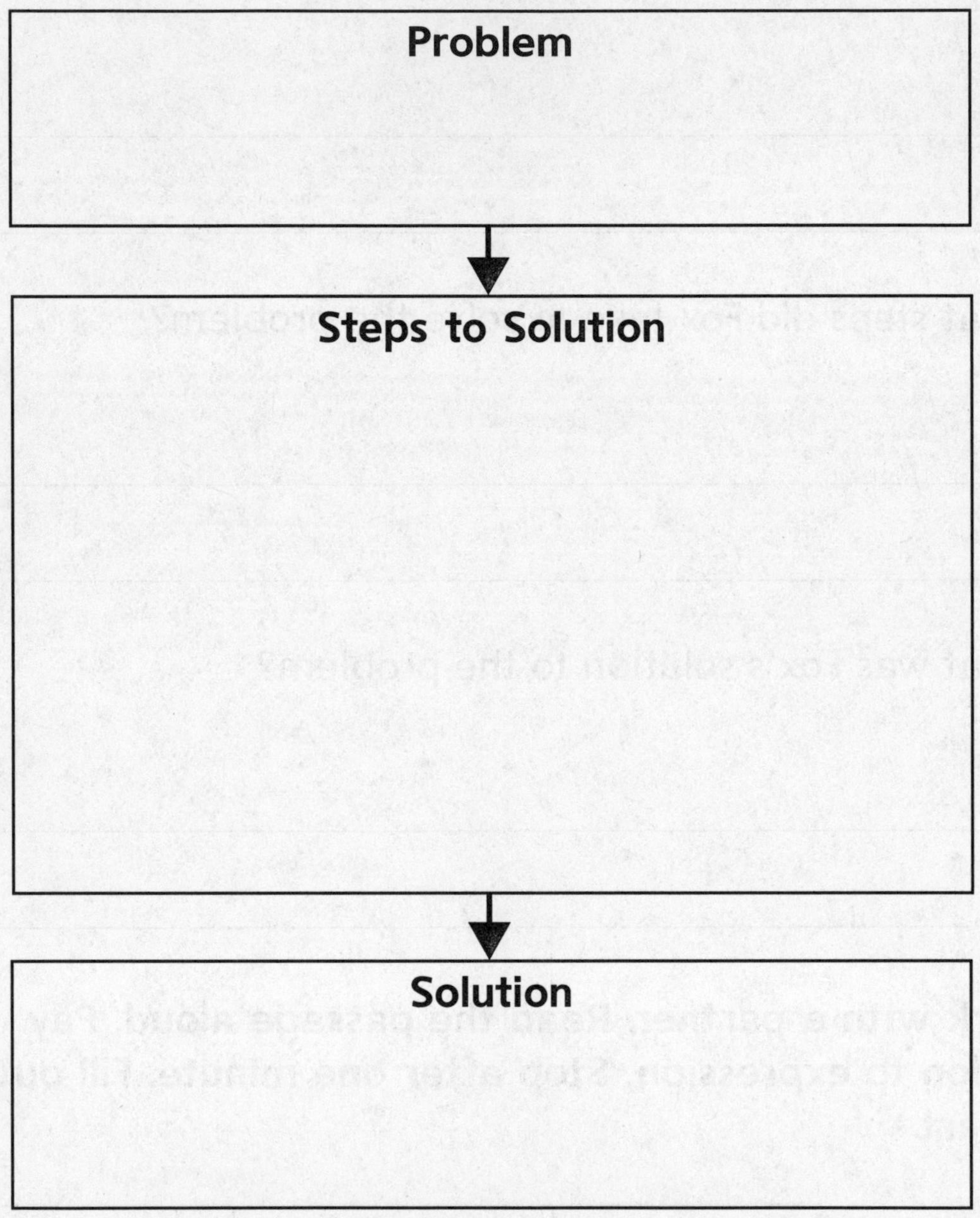

Name ____

The Fox and the Grapes

One day the fox saw a bunch of grapes high in a tree. He could not reach the grapes. The fox walked away. "Those grapes must be sour," he said. It is easy to dislike something you cannot get.

Answer the questions about the text.

1. How can you tell that this text is a fable?

____

____

2. What happens at the beginning of the fable?

____

3. What happens at the end of the fable?

____

4. What lesson does the fable teach?

____

Name ____

To figure out a new word, look for a **suffix**, or word part added to the end of the word.

The suffix ***-ful*** means "full of."

The suffix ***-ly*** means "in a way that is."

Read each sentence. Underline the word that has a suffix. Then write the word and its meaning.

1. "Those will make a healthful snack," Fox thought.

____

2. He should be able to reach the grapes easily.

____

3. The wind began blowing strongly.

____

4. Turtle had an idea that was helpful.

____

5. When Fox was safely back on the ground, he shared the grapes with Turtle.

____

Name ______________________________

A. Read the draft model. Use the questions that follow the draft to help you add supporting details.

Draft Model

Every day a shepherd boy thought he saw a wolf. "Wolf!" he cried. The villagers came running. They felt sorry for the boy.

1. How does the shepherd boy feel?
2. What is he thinking about when he thinks he sees a wolf?
3. What details could explain more about the actions of the shepherd boy and the villagers?

B. Now revise the draft by adding supporting details that explain your ideas about how the shepherd boy and the villagers act, think, and feel.

____

____

____

____

____

____

Name ____________________

Mia used text evidence to answer the prompt: *Add an event to* Wolf! Wolf! *in which the old wolf and the goat help Cinderella go to the ball.*

The wolf and the goat are now good friends. They are always together. One day they were picking vegetables when Cinderella visited. She was sad because she had no friends. The wolf and the goat said she could help them pick vegetables. After that, they became good friends.

One day Cinderella said she wanted to go to the town dance, but she didn't have a dress. The wolf and the goat wanted to help. They made a beautiful dress out of dandelion flowers.

Cinderella danced with the handsome king. She was so excited, she ran to tell her friends. On the way, she lost a slipper. The king returned it to her, and they fell in love.

Reread the passage. Follow the directions below.

1. **Circle** the reason that the wolf and the goat became Cinderella's friend.

2. **Draw a box** around a sentence that Mia wrote that includes a time-order word or phrase.

3. **Underline** an idea that shows how the wolf and the goat are such good friends to Cinderella.

4. **Write** a plural noun that is used in the first paragraph.

____________________.

Name ____________________

buried	escape	habitat	journey
nature	peeks	restless	spies

A. Read each clue below. Then find the vocabulary word on the right that matches the clue. Draw a line from the clue to the word.

1. the outdoor world
2. takes a quick look
3. the natural place where an animal lives
4. get away
5. cannot stay still
6. a long trip
7. covered up in the ground
8. watches and sees something

a. habitat
b. escape
c. spies
d. buried
e. peeks
f. nature
g. journey
h. restless

B. Choose one vocabulary word from the box above. Write the word in a sentence of your own.

9. ____________________

____

Name ____________________

The *c* in ***cent*** stands for the /s/ sound. It is soft *c*. The *g* in ***germ*** stands for the /j/ sound. It is soft *g*.

A. Read each word in the box. Then write the words that belong in each list.

space	range	trace	cage	badge	ice

Soft *g*	**Soft *c***
1. ____________	**4.** ____________
2. ____________	**5.** ____________
3. ____________	**6.** ____________

A **prefix** is a word part added to the beginning of a word to make a new word.

- The prefix ***re-*** means "again."
- The prefixes ***un-*** and ***dis-*** mean "not" or "opposite of."

B. Read each word. Write its meaning.

7. dislike ____________ **8.** reuse ____________

9. unkind ____________ **10.** redo ____________

Name ____________________

Read the passage. Use the make predictions strategy to predict what you will learn.

Two Kinds of Tundra

The Arctic Tundra

3 Dr. Jones went to the **Arctic tundra**. It was very cold
14 with no trees. There were grasses and flowers. Dr. Jones
24 was hopeful that he would see animals. He made a
34 careful study of what he found.

40 In the sky, Dr. Jones saw playful **ravens** and **gulls**.
50 On the ground, he saw **gray wolves** and **Arctic**
59 **hares**. He knew that many of these animals had extra
69 fat. This was useful. It kept the animals warm during
79 the cold winter. Some of the animals slept while others
89 went south.

Name ____

91 **The Alpine Tundra**

94 The next trip Dr. Jones took was to the **alpine**
104 **tundra**. He was greatly interested in comparing the two
113 places. This tundra did not have trees, either. The alpine
123 plants were almost like the Arctic plants. The animals
132 were clearly different, though.

136 Dr. Jones saw birds such as **jays** and **grouse**. He saw
147 **sheep** and **elk**. He knew that some of these animals
157 also had extra fat. It kept them warm. Some of these
168 animals slept through the winter. Others went south.

Name ______________________________

A. Reread the passage and answer the questions.

1. What is the main topic of the passage?

____

____

2. What is a key detail about the Arctic tundra?

____

____

3. What is a key detail about the alpine tundra?

____

____

B. Work with a partner. Read the passage aloud. Pay attention to how you group words together as you read. Stop after one minute. Fill out the chart.

	Words Read	–	Number of Errors	=	Words Correct Score
First Read		–		=	
Second Read		–		=	

Name ____________________

Read the selection. Complete the Main Topic and Key Details chart.

Main Topic		
Detail	**Detail**	**Detail**

Name ________________________________

In the Cave

The scientist enters the cave. It is cold and dim. She spies **shrimp** and **cave beetles**. These animals never leave the cave. Then she sees a **snail**. It may leave the cave at times.

Cave Animals	
Always live in caves: cave shrimp, cave beetle, and cave fish.	Sometimes live in caves: snail, spider, and worm.

Answer the questions about the text.

1. How can you tell that this text is narrative nonfiction?

____

2. What happens after the scientist sees shrimp and cave beetles?

____

3. Why are **shrimp, cave beetles,** and **snail** in bold print?

____

4. What information can you get from the chart?

____

Name ____

To figure out a new word, look for a **suffix**, or word part added to the end of the word.

The suffix ***-ful*** means "full of."

The suffix ***-ly*** means "in a way that is."

A. Underline the word that has a suffix in each sentence. Then write the word and its meaning.

1. Dr. Jones was hopeful that he would see animals.

____

2. He made a careful study of what he found.

____

3. He was greatly interested in comparing the two places.

____

B. Write a word that means the same as the group of words. Your new word will end in *-ful* or *-ly*.

4. full of play

____

5. in way that is clear

____

Name ____

A. Read the draft model. Use the questions that follow the draft to help you add sequence words.

Draft Model

I saw a white tiger when I visited the zoo last summer. It was a very hot day, and the white tiger was panting. He splashed around in a lake that surrounded his pen. Caretakers threw him giant ice cubes. He licked and ate the cubes that contained fruit. He moved to a shady area of his pen.

1. What does the white tiger do first? What does he do next?

2. What event happens last?

3. What words can you add to make the writing easier to understand?

B. Now revise the draft by adding sequence words such as *first, next, then,* and *last* to help readers understand the order of events.

____

____

____

____

____

Name ____

Stella used text evidence to answer the prompt: *How are the turtles in both selections alike and different? Use details from both texts.*

The turtles in *Turtle, Turtle, Watch Out!* and "At Home in the River" are similar in many ways. They are also different in some ways.

On page 166 of *Turtle, Turtle, Watch Out!*, I read that the mother turtle covers her eggs with sand from the beach. The mother turtle from "At Home in the River" also covers her eggs. She covers them with dirt to protect them.

The turtles are different too. In *Turtle, Turtle, Watch Out!*, I read that the turtles are born in the sand and then swim to the ocean. The turtles in "At Home in the River" are born in the dirt, and then swim in the river.

The turtles are similar, and they are also different.

Reread the passage. Follow the directions below.

1. **Underline** the order of events from the ocean's turtle's birth to its return to the ocean.

2. **Draw a box** around text evidence from either selection.

3. **Circle** the sentence in which Stella sums up her ideas.

4. **Write** a common noun that is used in the third paragraph.

____.

Name ______________________________

adult	alive	covered	fur
giant	groom	mammal	offspring

Choose the word that makes sense in each blank. Then write the word on the line.

1. A baby chick is ______________ with soft feathers.
2. Some ______________ look a lot like their parents.
3. Whales are ______________ sea animals.
4. A cat will ______________ itself to stay clean.
5. A horse is a ______________ because it feeds its babies milk.
6. A fox's ______________ coat helps to keep it warm.
7. Some baby animals need to be cared for by an __________.
8. Animals need food and water to stay ______________.

Name ______________________________

A **consonant digraph** is two consonants together that stand for only one sound.

A. Say each picture name. Read the words and circle the word with the same beginning sound. Write the word.

1. chop sting ____________

2. pitch while ____________

A **suffix** is a word part added to the end of a word to make a new word.

- The suffix *-ful* means "full of."
- The suffix *-less* means "without."

B. Read each word. Write its meaning.

3. helpless ____________ 4. careful ____________

5. thankful ____________ 6. useless ____________

Name ______________________________

Read the passage. Use the reread strategy to make sure you understand the information.

Opossums

An adult opossum is about the size of a big cat. When
12 the mother gives birth, she may have seven or more
22 babies. She has a pouch like a kangaroo.

30 Each baby opossum is the size of a honeybee. At
40 first, they stay inside the mother's pouch. After about
49 two months, the babies leave the mother's pouch. They
58 are still small. The mother can carry the babies on her
69 back. The baby opossums grow quickly. Soon the young
78 animals are on their own.

Name ______________________________

Opossum

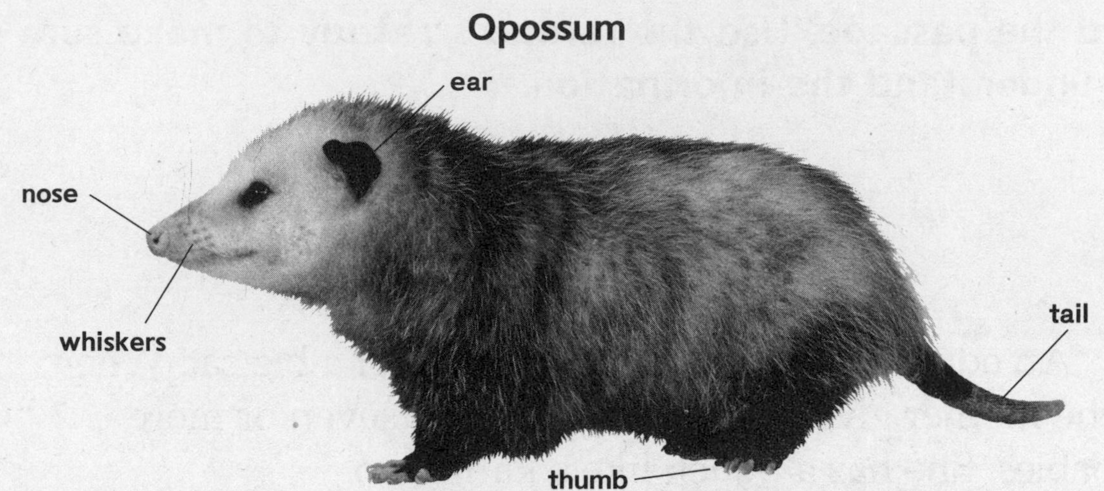

83 An adult opossum has long gray fur on its body.
93 Its face is white. It has black ears. The opossum has
104 a pointed snout with a pink nose. Its tail and feet are
116 pink, too. It has a mouth full of fifty sharp teeth.

127 An opossum has a very useful tail. This tail is almost
138 a foot long with very little hair. An opossum can use
149 this tail to grab onto things. Its tail helps it hold onto
161 tree branches. On each hind foot, an opossum has a
171 thumb. These thumbs help it grab onto things, too.

180 These animals are known for "playing possum."
187 When rattled by a predator, they lie still and don't move
198 at all until the threat goes away.

Name ______________________________

A. Reread the passage and answer the questions.

1. What is the main topic of the passage?

____

____

2. What is a key detail about an adult opossum?

____

____

3. What is a key detail about a baby opossum?

____

____

B. Work with a partner. Read the passage aloud. Pay attention to pronunciation. Stop after one minute. Fill out the chart.

	Words Read	–	Number of Errors	=	Words Correct Score
First Read		–		=	
Second Read		–		=	

Name ____

Read the selection. Complete the Main Topic and Key Details chart.

Main Topic		
Detail	**Detail**	**Detail**

Name ______________________________

Leopards and Their Cubs

Leopard cubs are born with their eyes closed. Their fur is longer and thicker than their parents' fur. It is grayer, too. The cubs' spots are not easy to see.

Leopard

Answer the questions about the text.

1. How do you know this is an expository text?

____

____

2. What information can you learn from looking at the diagram?

____

3. What information can you learn by reading the labels?

____

Name ____

Multiple-meaning words have more than one meaning. Use other words in the sentence to figure out which meaning is being used.

Read each sentence. Figure out the meaning of the word in bold print. Put a checkmark in the box before the meaning that matches its use in the sentence.

1. The mother can carry the babies on her **back**.
   - ☐ the part of the body opposite the front
   - ☐ to move away from something

2. The opossum has a **pointed** snout with a pink nose.
   - ☐ having a sharp end
   - ☐ showed where something is

3. Soon the young animals are on their **own**.
   - ☐ to have or hold as property
   - ☐ for or by oneself

4. When **rattled** by a predator, they lie still and don't move at all until the threat goes away.
   - ☐ made upset or disturbed
   - ☐ made noise

Name ____

A. Read the draft model. Use the questions that follow the draft to help you add linking words.

Draft Model

A puppy is the name for a baby dog. A puppy is much smaller than its parent. It is the same shape as its parent. It has fur like its parent. It cannot do many things for itself.

1. What are some ways you can connect the ideas in the draft?

2. How is a puppy different from its parent?

3. How is a puppy the same as its parent?

B. Now revise the draft by adding and replacing words to connect ideas with linking words, such as *and, so, also, but,* or *however*.

____

____

____

____

____

____

Name ______________________________

Nick used text evidence to answer the prompt: *Which selection is presented in a more clear and understandable manner?*

I think that *Baby Bears* presents information more clearly than "From Caterpillar to Butterfly." Both selections tell how baby animals become adults, but they are organized in different ways. I like the pictures in *Baby Bears* to see the differences between bear cubs and adults.

Both passages use diagrams to show how the animals change, but *Baby Bears* has more information to share. For example, it tells about the eight kinds of bears on page 190. On the next page, the text gives more detailed information about one kind of bear, the panda. In "From Caterpillar to Butterfly" the butterfly and its offspring are the only topic. The focus is the life cycle, with little information on the kinds of butterflies.

Reread the passage. Follow the directions below.

1. Nick states his opinion in the topic sentence. **Underline** the topic sentence.
2. Nick includes facts about bears and butterflies in his response. **Draw a box** around one of the facts.
3. **Circle** a linking word that Nick uses to connect ideas.
4. **Write** a noun from the model that changes its spelling from singular to plural.

______________________________.

Name ____________________

behave	express
feathers	flapping

Use what you know about the words in the sentences to choose the word that makes sense in each blank. Then write the word on the line.

1. The crow has black ______.

____

2. The bird is able to fly by ______ its wings.

____

3. The children ______ by following the classroom rules.

____

4. I ______ myself by writing in a journal.

____

B. Choose one vocabulary word from the box above. Write the word in a sentence of your own.

5. ____

____

Name ____________________

Three letters can be blended together such as ***scr, spl, spr, str, shr,*** and ***thr.*** Listen to the beginning sounds in ***scrap*** and ***split***.

A. Look at the picture. Write the missing blend for each word.

1.  ________one

2.  ________ash

3.  ________ub

4. 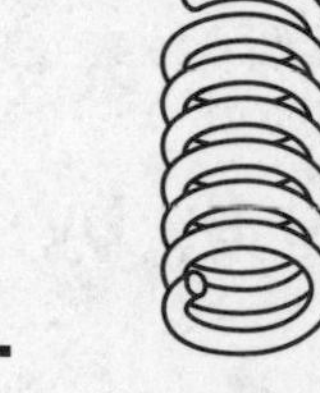 ________ing

5.  ________ap

6.  ________ub

A **compound word** is made up of two smaller words.

B. Circle each compound word. Write the two smaller words that make it up.

7. beaches bedspread ____________ ____________

8. wishbone wonder ____________ ____________

9. springtime spotted ____________ ____________

Name ____

Read the poem. Use the reread strategy to check your understanding.

A Tortoise

You will find that a tortoise is a mild fellow,
10 It lives a life that's calm and mellow.

18 A tortoise can live for quite a long span,
27 In fact it may even live longer than a man.

37 You'll never find a tortoise at sea,
44 It lives on land—that's where it should be.

53 Would a tortoise be able to win a race?
62 Not since it moves at such a slow pace.

71 It has four stumpy legs and four tortoise feet.
80 For a snack, plants are its favorite of treat.

Name ______________________________

89 Some creatures have feathers and some have hair,
97 But what does our friend tortoise wear?

104 A tortoise wears a hard outer shell,
111 That always works to serve it well.

118 When a tortoise doesn't know where to hide,
126 It just pulls its head and four limbs inside.

135 Even though a tortoise may be shy,
142 It can walk around with its head held high.

151 For a tortoise is a marvel of the animal pack,
161 It carries its home right on its back.

Name ________________________________

A. Reread the passage and answer the questions.

1. How long can a tortoise live?

____

____

2. Where does a tortoise live?

____

____

3. How does a tortoise use its shell?

____

____

B. Work with a partner. Read the passage aloud. Pay attention to how you pause and group words together. Stop after one minute. Fill out the chart.

	Words Read	–	Number of Errors	=	Words Correct Score
First Read		–		=	
Second Read		–		=	

Name ____

Read the selection. Complete the Key Details chart.

Detail	Detail	Detail

Name ____

The Robin

A robin gathers twigs and fluff,
And sticks and string and other stuff.
She chooses things she likes the best,
And weaves them in to build her nest.

Answer the questions about the text.

1. How do you know this text is a poem?

____

____

2. How many beats do you hear in each line?

____

____

3. Why do you think the poet uses rhythm?

____

____

Name ____

Multiple-meaning words have more than one meaning. Use other words in the sentence to figure out which meaning is being used.

Read the lines from the poem. Circle the meaning of the word in bold print.

1. You'll never find a tortoise at sea,
It lives on **land**—that's where it should be.

the ground   to come down from above

2. A tortoise wears a hard outer shell,
That always works to serve it **well**.

in a good way   a hole in the ground that stores water

3. It has four stumpy legs and four tortoise **feet**.

measurements of 12 inches   parts of the body

4. When a tortoise doesn't know where to hide,
It just pulls its head and four **limbs** inside.

tree branches   legs

5. For a tortoise is a marvel of the animal **pack**,
It carries its home right on its back.

to put things in a suitcase   a group of animals

Name ______________________________

A. Read the draft model. Use the questions that follow the draft to help you think about what precise words you can add.

Draft Model

I went outside one night.
Something moved, so I turned on the light.
It was a little toad,
Hopping across the road.

1. What kind of night is it?

2. What does the toad look like?

3. How does the toad move?

B. Now revise the draft by adding precise words to give readers a clearer picture about the night and the toad.

____

____

____

____

____

Name ____________________

Martin used text evidence to answer the prompt: *Write a poem about an animal that is very busy. Use precise words and rhyme.*

Noisy Fly

A noisy fly flew into my room.
Just like an airplane's motor, it went *zoom zoom zoom.*
It buzzed by my nose and landed on the wall.
Then it swooshed up to the ceiling and started to fall.
Down it went to the floor with a boom.
Buzzing, buzzing...
"Noisy fly, get out of my room!"

Reread the passage. Follow the directions below.

1. **Draw a box** around a specific word that Martin uses that tells how the fly was busy.

2. **Circle** two words from the poem that rhyme.

3. Martin adds details about how the fly sounded. **Underline** a detail that tells how it sounded.

4. **Write** an example of a possessive noun from the model.

____________________.

Name ____________________

amazing	force	measure	objects
proved	speed	true	weight

A. Read each clue below. Then find the vocabulary word on the right that matches the clue. Draw a line from the clue to the word.

1. how heavy something is	a. speed
2. showed something is true	b. amazing
3. very surprising	c. weight
4. how fast something moves	d. force
5. not false	e. proved
6. things you can see and touch	f. measure
7. a push or a pull	g. objects
8. find the size of something	h. true

B. Choose one vocabulary word from the box above. Write the word in a sentence of your own.

9. ____________________

____

Name ______________________________

The letters ***a, ai, ay, ea, ei, eigh,*** and ***ey*** can stand for the long ***a*** sound. Listen to the vowel sound as you say the words ***apron, pail, day, great, eight,*** and ***they***.

A. Read each row of words. Circle the long *a* word and write it on the line. Then underline the letters that spell the long *a* sound.

1. bike jump stay ______________
2. camp nail green ______________
3. weigh mean lock ______________
4. shell prey huge ______________
5. rein rope pick ______________
6. float break last ______________
7. snap pump baby ______________

A **contraction** is a short way of writing two words. An apostrophe stands for the missing letters.

B. Write the contraction for each pair of words.

8. they have ______________ 9. she is ______________

10. we are ______________ 11. you will ______________

Name ______________________________

Read the passage. Use the reread strategy to check your understanding of new information or difficult facts.

Roller Coaster Science

Riding a roller coaster can feel like flying. The cars
10 race up and down the track. They go around corners at
21 a high speed. Do you know how a roller coaster works?

32 **The Ride Begins**

35 A long chain runs under the first uphill track. A
45 motor moves this chain in a loop. It's like the moving
56 belt at the store checkout. The roller coaster cars grip
66 onto the chain. The chain pulls the roller coaster train
76 up to the top of the hill.

83 **Moving Along the Track**

87 The train reaches the top of the hill. The chain is
98 unhooked. **Gravity** takes the train down the track.
106 Gravity is a **force** that pulls objects toward the center of
117 the earth.

Name ______________________________

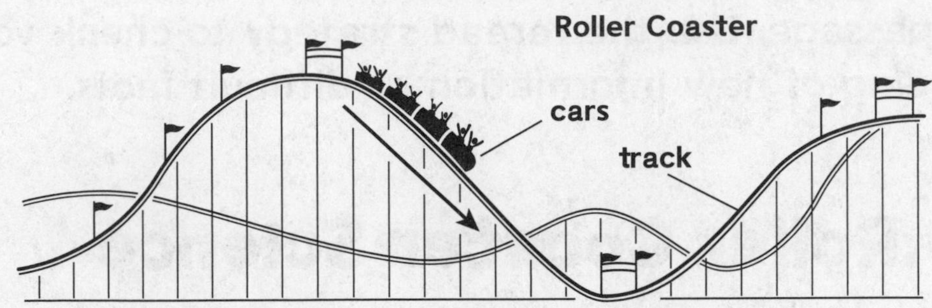

Gravity moves the cars down the hill.

119 As the train moves down the track, it **speeds** up. It
130 goes faster and faster. This speed helps move the train
140 up the next hill. Then it all happens again.

149 **The Ride Ends**

152 When the ride is over, the roller coaster train must
162 stop. There are brakes built into the track. These brakes
172 stop the **motion** of the train. The roller coaster ends at
183 the same position it started.

188 That is the science of a roller coaster. Think about
198 these forces the next time you take a ride!

Name ______________________________

A. Reread the passage and answer the questions.

1. What is the topic of this passage?

____

____

2. What is one fact that the author includes about the topic?

____

____

3. What is the author's purpose for writing this passage?

____

____

B. Work with a partner. Read the passage aloud. Pay attention to how your voice rises and falls. Stop after one minute. Fill out the chart.

	Words Read	–	Number of Errors	=	Words Correct Score
First Read		–		=	
Second Read		–		=	

Name ______________________________

Read the selection. Complete the Author's Purpose chart.

Clue	**Clue**

Author's Purpose

Name ______________________________

How a Yo-Yo Works

Let a yo-yo go and it spins down as the string **unwinds**. It keeps spinning at the end of the string. With a quick tug, the string **rewinds** and the yo-yo climbs back up.

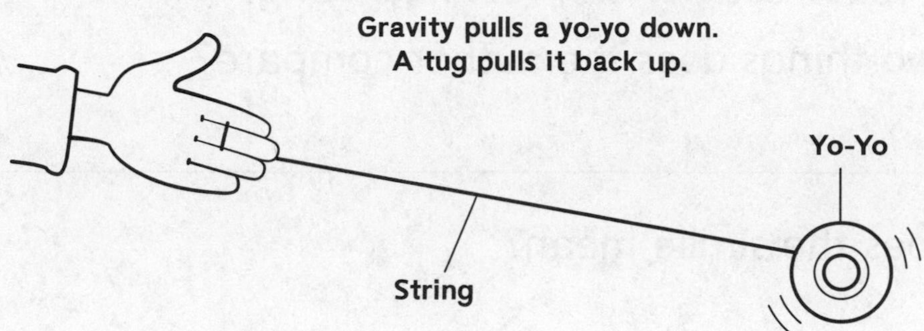

Answer the questions about the text.

1. How do you know this is informational text?

____

____

2. Why are the words **unwinds** and **rewinds** in bold print?

____

____

3. What can you learn from the diagram?

____

Name ______________________________

A **simile** compares two unlike things. It uses the word *like* or *as* to make the comparison.

Read the sentences. Then answer the questions.

1. Riding a roller coaster can feel like flying.

   What two things does the author compare?

   ____

   What does the simile mean?

   ____

   ____

2. A motor moves this chain in a loop. It is like the moving belt at the store checkout.

   What two things does the author compare?

   ____

   What does the simile mean?

   ____

3. The roller coaster's sound is as loud as thunder.

   What two things does the author compare?

   ____

   What does the simile mean?

   ____

Name ____________________

A. Read the draft model. Use the questions that follow the draft to add words that tell the order of the ideas.

Draft Model

You use the force of push and pull. When you throw the ball to a player, you use the force of push. When you try to take the ball from a player, you use the force of pull.

1. What words can you add to the first sentence to make it clearer?

2. What words can you add to the second sentence to make it clearer?

3. Does the order of ideas make sense?

B. Now revise the draft by adding words. Check that the order of ideas makes sense.

____

____

____

____

____

____

Name ____

Paul used text evidence to answer the prompt: *How are motion and gravity related?*

> Motion and gravity are related because they both cause things to move. Gravity is a force that pulls things towards Earth. On page 215 of "I Fall Down," the author explains, "gravity is always pulling things" and they always fall down. In "Move It!," I read that motion is a change in position.
>
> In "Move It!," I learned that things need the "push or pull of a different force" to move. On page 231, I read that a soccer ball needs to be kicked or thrown if it is going to move. Because of gravity, if you kick a soccer ball up in the air, it will always fall back to Earth. Motion and gravity work together all the time to move things and bring them back to Earth.

Reread the passage. Follow the directions below.

1. **Draw a box** around a sentence that tells how gravity works when you kick a soccer ball in the air.

2. **Circle** a fact from "I Fall Down" that supports Paul's answer.

3. **Underline** the sentence that sums up Paul's response.

4. **Write** an action verb that Paul uses.

____.

Name ____

adventure	delighted	dreamed	enjoyed
grumbled	moonlight	neighbor	nighttime

Read the story. Choose words from the box to complete the sentences. Then write the answers on the lines.

The sky got dark when ______________ came. Max ______________ that the end of the day was boring.

"Let's take a walk outside," said Mom. "The stars and ______________ can light our way."

They walked down the street. Max was surprised and ______________ to see an owl fly by. They passed the house of a ______________. There was a light shining in each window.

Max and Mom returned home. "What did you think of our night ______________?" asked Mom.

"I really ______________ it," said Max. I never ______________ that night could be exciting!"

Name ______________________________

The letters ***i, y, igh,*** and ***ie*** can stand for the long *i* sound. Listen to the vowel sound as you say the words ***kind, why, might,*** and ***skies***.

A. Write the words in the box in the correct list below.

cry	light	wild	tie	high
sight	lie	dry	mind	try

1. words with the long *i* sound, as in *find*

__________ __________

2. words with the long *i* sound, as in *fly*

__________ __________ __________

3. words with the long *i* sound, as in *bright*

__________ __________ __________

4. words with the long *i* sound, as in *pie*

__________ __________

B. Draw a line to divide each word into syllables.

5. pony

6. table

7. spider

8. music

Name ____

Read the passage. Use the reread strategy to check your understanding of story events.

A Shooting Star

Carla's family got to the park in the late afternoon.
10 The sun was shining in the blue sky. There was not a
22 cloud anywhere.

24 Carla and her sister Rosa were excited. It was their
34 first camping trip. They ran around the campsite. They
43 saw lots of big evergreen trees. A chipmunk ran on a
54 branch overhead.

56 Mama said, "Let's get things set up. Then we can go
67 for a hike."

70 Papa added, "We should have enough time to hike
79 before nightfall."

81 After the tents were set up, the family hiked. Daylight
91 was fading as they returned to the campsite.

99 "Look! There are fireflies here," said Carla.

Name ________________________________

106 Everyone looked up to watch the fireflies. Just then,
115 they saw a shooting star cross the dark night sky.

125 "What is that?" Rosa asked.

130 "It's a shooting star. Some people say you can wish
140 on a shooting star and your wish will come true,"
150 said Papa.

152 Carla and Rosa quickly made wishes.

158 Mama explained, "Some people call it a shooting star.
167 It's not a star, though. It's really just some dust flying
178 toward the earth. It heats up and glows. That's what
188 we see."

190 "No matter what we call it, I hope our wishes come
201 true!" said Carla.

Name ______________________________

A. Reread the passage and answer the questions.

1. What happens first in the story?

____

____

2. What happens after it gets dark?

____

____

3. What happens last?

____

____

B. Work with a partner. Read the passage aloud. Pay attention to how your voice rises and falls. Stop after one minute. Fill out the chart.

	Words Read	–	Number of Errors	=	Words Correct Score
First Read		–		=	
Second Read		–		=	

Name ______________________________

Read the selection. Complete the Sequence chart.

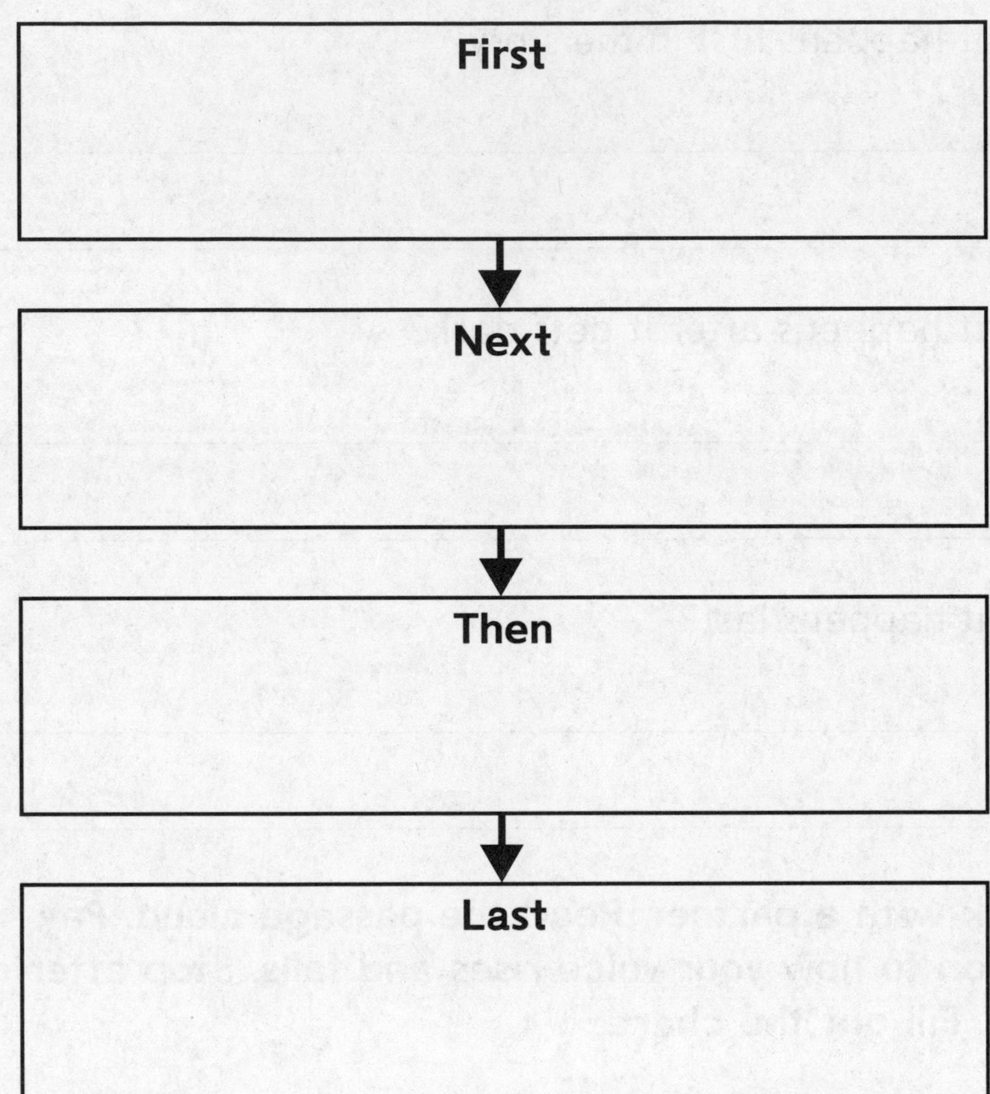

Name ___________________________

Shapes in the Sky

One day, two friends named the cloud shapes they saw.

"Look at all the clouds in the sky. That one looks like a lion," said Grace.

"That cloud looks like a train," Marco said.

Answer the questions about the text.

1. How do you know this text is fiction?

____

2. What is dialogue?

____

3. What words does Grace say?

____

4. What words does Marco say?

____

Name ______________________________

A **compound word** is a word made of two smaller words.

A. Read each sentence. Write the compound word. Draw a line between the two smaller words.

1. There was not a cloud anywhere. ______________

2. They ran around the campsite. ______________

3. They saw lots of big evergreen trees. ______________

4. There are fireflies here. ______________

B. Write the meaning of each compound word.

5. afternoon

____

6. daylight

____

7. everyone

____

8. nightfall

____

Name ______________________________

A. Read the draft model. Use the questions that follow the draft to help you add words to connect ideas.

Draft Model

James and Dad were camping. The moonlight was bright. It shone on their tent. He saw the Big Dipper. The night was so dark. James dreamed he took a rocket ship so he could see more stars.

1. Which sentence already has a linking word in it?
2. What sentences can be combined to connect ideas?
3. What are some words you can use to show how the ideas are connected?

B. Now revise the draft by adding and replacing words to connect ideas with linking words, such as *and, so, but,* or *because.*

____

____

____

____

____

____

Name ______________________________

Amelia used text evidence to answer the prompt: *Write a descriptive piece where Mr. Putter and Mrs. Teaberry watch a sunset together.*

Fluffy clouds fill the sky. The sun is just beginning to set, and the clouds turn soft orange, then pink, then deep red. The sun is a glowing ball, disappearing behind the clouds.

The two friends talk about the sunset, admiring its beauty. Mr. Putter tells how the sun is just a lot of hot gases. It looks like it moves all day, he says, but it is really Earth that moves. They talk of how much they like watching the sky. Then Mrs. Teaberry tells him she has always wanted to travel into space.

Mr. Putter listens quietly. He thought of the things he would miss if he traveled into space, including Mrs. Teaberry.

Reread the passage. Follow the directions below.

1. **Underline** the order of events in the sunset.

2. **Draw a box** around a detail that tells about the sun.

3. **Circle** a linking word that tells more about the sun.

4. **Write** a present-tense verb that Amelia used.

______________________________.

Name ______________________________

across	borrow	countryside	idea
insists	lonely	solution	villages

Choose the word that makes sense in each blank. Then write the word on the line.

1. The road passes through many small towns and __________.
2. We saw a sheep farm in the __________.
3. She felt __________ when everyone left the house.
4. May I please __________ your pencil?
5. The boy has a good __________ for his art project.
6. They use the bridge to get __________ the stream.
7. I know the __________ to this math problem.
8. The teacher __________ that students do their best.

Name ______________________________

The letters ***o, oa, ow,*** and ***oe*** can stand for the long ***o*** sound. Listen to the vowel sound as you say the words ***so, road, low,*** and ***woe***.

A. Read each word in the box. Circle the words with the long *o* sound. Then underline the letter or letters that spell the long *o* sound.

drop	coat	told	mow	book
most	grow	loop	Joe	lost
toast	pond	show	toe	float

A **contraction** is a short way of writing two words. An apostrophe stands for the missing letters.

B. Write the two words that make up each contraction.

1. isn't ________________ **2.** didn't ________________

3. won't ________________ **4.** aren't ________________

Name ______________________________

Read the passage. Ask and answer questions as you read to check your understanding.

Helping Out in the Community

Doug Long has been riding bikes for a long time.
10 When he was 16, he took a solo bike trip. He rode his
23 bike alone across the United States. That's a big journey
33 for a young man!

37 Now when Doug rides, it may be with a group of
48 children. Doug works with a volunteer group. The group
57 sets up bike rides for city kids. It gives the children time
69 to appreciate and enjoy the world around them. Doug
78 helps them explore nature.

82 Doug brings his own bike and helmet for a bike trip.
93 The children get bikes to ride and helmets to wear. Then
104 they go to a park or a nature area.

Name ____

Doug Long helps children learn more about nature.

113 On one trip, the children saw a caterpillar. They
122 weren't sure if it was safe to touch it. Doug picked it up.
135 He showed it to the children. Once they were certain it
146 was harmless, they all took turns holding it.

154 Between bike trips, the children can learn how to fix
164 bikes. They can work at a bike workshop. This earns
174 them points. They can use the points to get a bike of
186 their own.

188 Doug Long likes to ride his bike. And he likes to help
200 out. He has made his community a better place.

Photo Courtesy of Doug Long and Trips for Kids

Name ____

A. Reread the passage and answer the questions.

1. What did the author want you to know about Doug Long when Doug was 16?

____

____

2. What did the author want you to know about Doug's work with a volunteer group?

____

____

3. What is the author's purpose for writing this passage?

____

____

B. Work with a partner. Read the passage aloud. Pay attention to how you show feelings with your voice. Stop after one minute. Fill out the chart.

	Words Read	–	Number of Errors	=	Words Correct Score
First Read		–		=	
Second Read		–		=	

Name ______________________________

Read the selection. Complete the Author's Purpose chart.

Clue	**Clue**

Author's Purpose

Name ______________________________

A Friendly City for Bikes

Sara Krause lives in Austin, Texas. The mayor asked her for ideas to improve bike safety. Now Sara and many other people have helped make Austin a friendly city for bikes.

Sara Krause was the leader of the bike safety group in Austin.

Answer the questions about the text.

1. How can you tell that this text is narrative nonfiction?

____

____

2. How has Sara Krause helped out in Austin?

____

____

3. Why does the author include a photo?

____

4. What information can you learn from the caption?

____

____

Name ____________________

Synonyms are words that have almost the same meaning.

A. Read each pair of sentences. Find the two words that are synonyms. Circle the synonyms and then write them on the lines.

1. When he was 16, he took a solo bike trip.
   He rode his bike alone across the United States.

   ____________________ ____________________

2. When he was 16, he took a solo bike trip.
   That's a big journey for a young man!

   ____________________ ____________________

3. Now when Doug rides, it may be with a group of children.
   The group sets up bike rides for city kids.

   ____________________ ____________________

B. Read the sentences. Write a word to answer each question.

They weren't sure if it was safe to touch it.
Once they were certain it was harmless, they all took turns holding it.

4. Which word in the second sentence is a synonym for **sure**?

   ____

5. Which word in the second sentence is a synonym for **safe**?

   ____

Name ______________________________

A. Read the draft model. Use the questions that follow the draft to help you add opinion words and phrases.

Draft Model

Last week my family went to the park. There was trash on the ground. We told friends and neighbors. We all helped clean it up. Now the park is nicer.

1. How do you think the writer feels about seeing trash at the park?
2. Why does everyone help clean up the trash?
3. How does everyone feel once the park is cleaned up?

B. Now revise the draft by adding opinion words and phrases to show how the writer feels about the topic.

____

____

____

____

____

____

____

Name ____

Timmothy used text evidence to answer the prompt: *Who do you think had the bigger problem to solve, Luis or the farmer?*

I think Luis had the bigger problem to solve. His idea of sharing his books with people in faraway lands was difficult. He had to travel far. He had to leave his wife. Although two burros carried the books, one burro would not cross a stream. Luis had to pull and pull on the reins to get the burro to move.

The farmer in "The Enormous Turnip" had grown a huge turnip. His problem was that he cannot pull it out of the ground. In the end, the villagers helped the farmer and his family solve his problem. They all pulled the turnip out of the ground.

I think I will have a job like Luis one day, traveling to faraway lands to help people. That will be a good problem!

Reread the passage. Follow the directions below.

1. **Circle** the sentence that states Timmothy's opinion.
2. **Draw a box** around a reason that support Timmothy's opinion.
3. **Underline** a sentence that Timmothy added to sum up his opinion.
4. **Write** a future-tense verb on the line.

____.

Name ______________________________

damage	dangerous	destroy	event
harsh	prevent	warning	weather

A. Use what you know about the definitions to choose the word that makes sense for each clue. Write the word on the line.

1. a sign of danger to come ____________________

2. something that happens ____________________

3. injury or harm that happens to something

____

4. what it is like outside at a certain time and place

____

5. to stop something from happening ____________________

6. not safe ____________________

7. rough or unpleasant ____________________

8. to break something so it can't be used ____________________

B. Choose one vocabulary word from the box above. Write the word in a sentence of your own.

9. ____

Name ______________________________

The letters ***e, ee, ea, ie, y, ey,*** and ***e_e*** can stand for the long ***e*** sound. Listen to the vowel sound as you say the words ***me, see, leap, field, happy, money,*** and ***eve***.

A. Read each row of words. Circle the long *e* word and write it on the line. Then underline the letters that spell the long *e* sound.

1. must leaf sleigh ____________
2. chief track vase ____________
3. bee rest home ____________
4. they drum pony ____________
5. steak we block ____________
6. keys spend wise ____________

Add *-s* to form the plural of most nouns.

If a word ends in a consonant plus *y,* change the *y* to *i* and add *-es* to form the plural.

B. Write each word to make it plural.

7. puppy ____________
8. clock ____________
9. baby ____________
10. nest ____________

Name ____

Read the passage. Ask and answer questions as you read to check your understanding.

Ice Hotels

How would you like to stay in an ice hotel? There
11 really are such places in cold climates.

18 **What Is an Ice Hotel?**

23 An ice hotel is like a big **igloo**. The walls are made of
36 snow and ice. The furniture and art are made of ice, too.

48 **How Is an Ice Hotel Built?**

54 In some cold places, people build ice hotels. They
63 wait until winter because summer is too warm. Builders
72 choose a spot near a frozen river. Workers cut many ice
83 blocks to build walls. They use **snice** to keep the blocks
94 from coming apart. This is a mix of snow and ice that
106 holds everything together.

109 When they are done with the outside walls, workers
118 move to the inside. They carve furniture from blocks
127 of ice. They carve works of art, too. All this work takes
139 time. A large ice hotel can take five to six weeks to build.

Name ______________________________

152 **Staying in an Ice Hotel**

157 People must bundle up to stay in an ice hotel. The
168 **temperature** inside must stay below freezing. If it gets
177 above freezing, the ice could melt.

183 People sleep in thick sleeping bags on ice beds. They
193 sit on ice chairs. They even drink from ice glasses.

203 **What Happens to an Ice Hotel?**

209 An ice hotel only stands while it is cold. Once spring
220 comes, the hotel melts. The water returns to the river.
230 Then builders must wait until winter when the water
239 freezes to build the next ice hotel.

Name ______________________________

A. Reread the passage and answer the questions.

1. What is one key detail from the passage?

____

____

2. What is another key detail from the passage?

____

____

3. What is the main idea of the passage?

____

____

B. Work with a partner. Read the passage aloud. Pay attention to where you pause. Stop after one minute. Fill out the chart.

	Words Read	–	Number of Errors	=	Words Correct Score
First Read		–		=	
Second Read		–		=	

Name ____

Read the selection. Complete the Main Idea and Key Details chart.

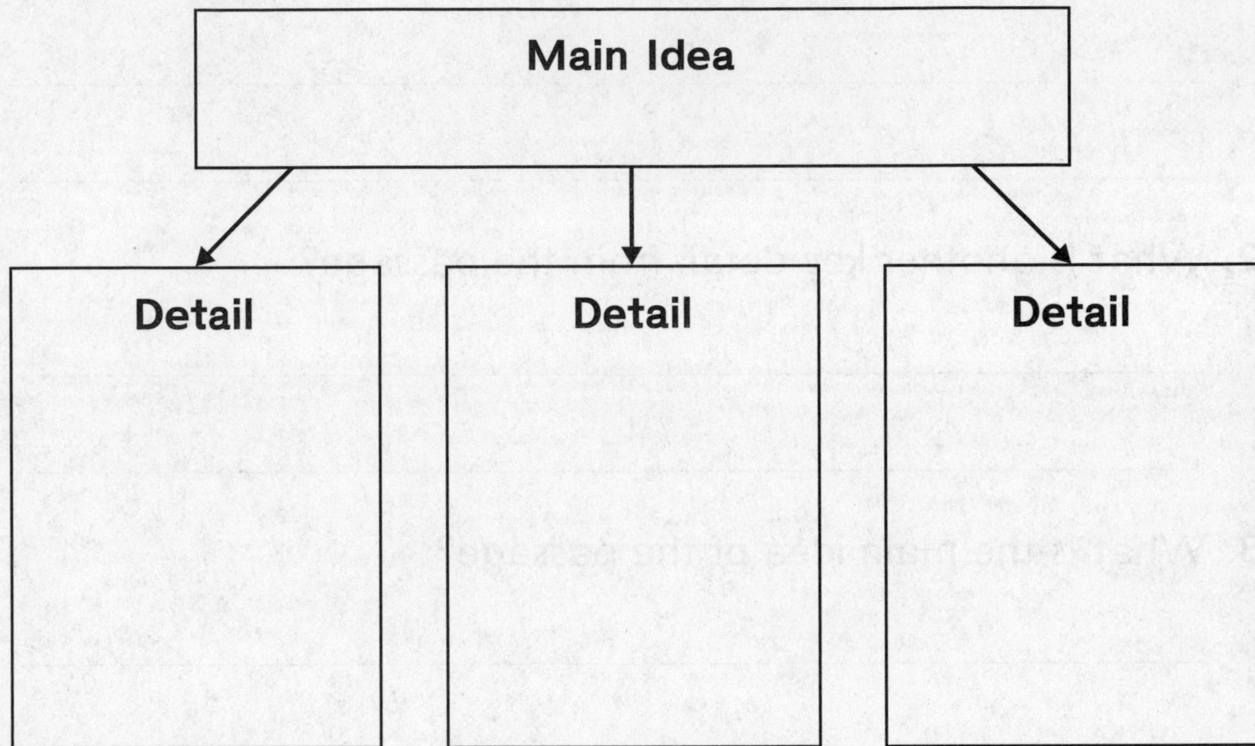

Name ______________________________

Drought

A **drought** is a long period of dry weather. Little or no rain falls during a drought. Without water, farmers' crops stop growing. The **water supply** for people gets low, too.

What to Do in a Drought
1. Use only the water you need.
2. Make sure there are no leaky faucets.
3. Take shorter showers.
4. Water outdoor plants and lawns when it is cold.

Answer the questions about the text.

1. How do you know that this is expository text?

____

____

2. Why are the words **drought** and **water supply** in bold print?

____

____

3. What can you learn from the sidebar?

____

Name ____

Antonyms are words that have opposite meanings.

A. Read each pair of sentences. Find the two words that are antonyms. Circle the antonyms and then write them on the lines.

1. They use snice to keep the blocks from coming apart. This is a mix of snow and ice that holds everything together.

   ____________________ ____________________

2. The workers finish the outside walls. Then they move to the inside.

   ____________________ ____________________

3. The shelf above the bed is made of ice. There is more ice below the bed.

   ____________________ ____________________

4. Once spring comes, the hotel melts. Then builders must wait until winter when the water freezes to build the next ice hotel.

   ____________________ ____________________

Name ____

A. Read the draft model. Use the questions that follow the draft to help you add a strong conclusion.

Draft Model

A weather forecaster tells people about the weather in the area. She tells how hot or cold it is. She can also warn about bad weather.

1. What is the topic of the writing?

2. What is the main idea?

3. What information could you include in a conclusion sentence?

B. Now revise the draft by adding a strong conclusion to sum up the writing and tell the main idea.

____

____

____

____

____

____

____

Name ____

Andrew used text evidence to answer the prompt: *Write about how scientists can predict a blizzard.*

Blizzards are winter storms with heavy snow and cold temperatures. They can be very dangerous. I see on page 288 of "Wild Weather" that snow in a blizzard can be very deep.

Meteorologists are the first scientists to track a blizzard. They have many tools, including radar, to track the storms. Meteorologists can see a storm that is coming on radar. In "Can You Predict the Weather?" I read that radar can warn people of the speed and direction of a storm.

Weather forecasters warn of big storms like blizzards on the radio, television, and even the Internet. Weather is all around us, but scientists can help us stay safe.

Reread the passage. Follow the directions below.

1. **Circle** an event that Andrew learned from a photo.
2. **Underline** a fact about a blizzard.
3. **Draw a box** around the ending that Andrew used to organize his writing.
4. **Write** a sentence on the line that includes the verb *have.*

____.

Name ______________________________

cheered	concert	instruments	movements
music	rhythm	sounds	understand

Use what you know about the words in the sentences to choose the word that makes sense in each blank. Then write the word on the line.

1. A swimmer kicks with strong leg ______________.

2. My sister listens to country ______________.

3. The band played my favorite song at the ______________.

4. I use a dictionary if I don't ______________ a word.

5. Pianos are ______________ that have keys.

6. He taps the ______________ of the song on his drum.

7. The rusty wheel made squeaking ______________ as it turned.

8. The crowd ______________ for their favorite team.

Name ________________________________

The letters ***u_e, ew, ue,*** and ***u*** can stand for the long ***u*** sound. Listen to the vowel sound as you say the words ***use, mew, hue,*** and ***menu.***

A. Read each word in the box. Circle the words with the long *u* sound. Then underline the letter or letters that spell the long *u* sound.

fuel	mule	just	few	bunch
cues	unit	jump	trunk	fumes
lucky	music	cube	pew	huge

The ending ***-er*** is added to an adjective to compare two nouns. The ending ***-est*** is added to an adjective to compare more than two nouns.

B. Write each word and ending to make a new word. Write it on the lines.

1. strong + est

   ____

2. few + er

   ____

3. kind + er

   ____

4. slow + est

   ____

Name ____

Read the passage. Ask and answer questions as you read to check your understanding.

Making Music

There are different ways to make music. Let's learn
09 about some musical instruments. You might find some
17 of these in your school music group.

24 **Piano**

25 A piano is a musical instrument that has 88 keys. To
36 play the piano, you press keys on the keyboard. This
46 action moves wooden hammers. The hammers then hit
54 steel strings. The strings vibrate and make sound. When
63 the strings stop moving, the sound is discontinued.

71 **Violin**

72 A violin is in the string family of instruments. It is a
84 hollow wooden box. It has four strings running from top
94 to bottom. To play the violin, you pull the bow across
105 the strings. Or you can pluck the strings with a finger.
116 When the strings vibrate, they make sound.

Name ______________________________

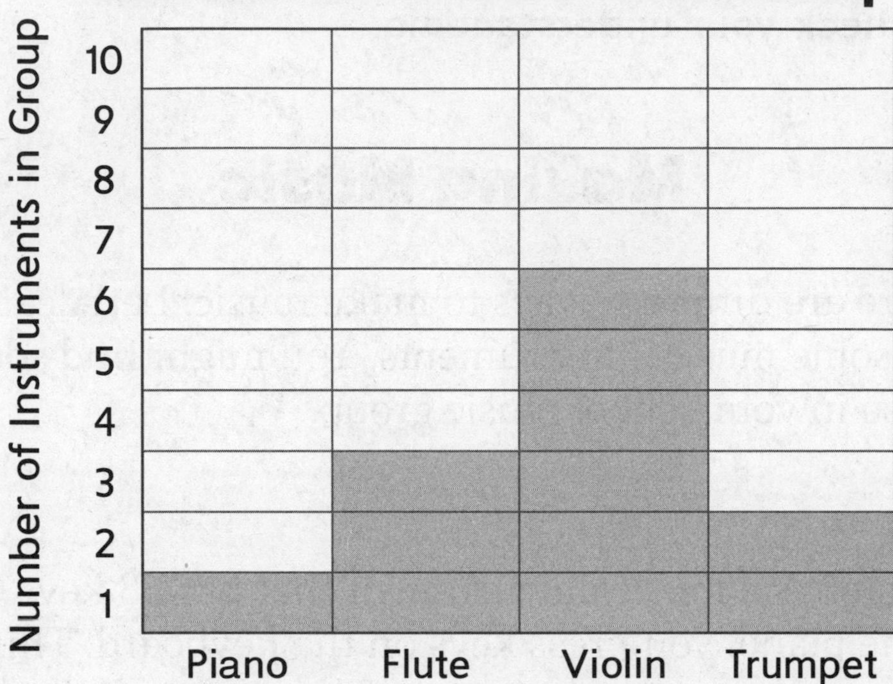

123 **Flute**

124 A flute is a woodwind instrument. It is a narrow tube
135 with finger holes. To make a sound on the flute, you
146 blow across an oval hole near the end. Sound bounces
156 off the edge of the hole and through the tube. To change
168 notes, cover and uncover the finger holes.

175 **Trumpet**

176 A trumpet is a brass instrument. It is a long, metal
187 tube with a loop. One end is shaped like a bell. It
199 has an uneven number of valves, three. To play the
209 trumpet, you buzz your lips into the mouthpiece. Move
218 the valves to change the notes.

224 Now let's review the instruments we read about.
232 Which would you like to play? No one can disagree.
242 There is a whole world of music to be made!

Name ____

A. Reread the passage and answer the questions.

1. What is one key detail that is included in the passage?

____

____

2. What is another key detail that is included in the passage?

____

____

3. What is the main idea of the passage?

____

____

B. Work with a partner. Read the passage aloud. Pay attention to pronunciation. Stop after one minute. Fill out the chart.

	Words Read	–	Number of Errors	=	Words Correct Score
First Read		–		=	
Second Read		–		=	

Name ____

Read the selection. Complete the Main Idea and Key Details chart.

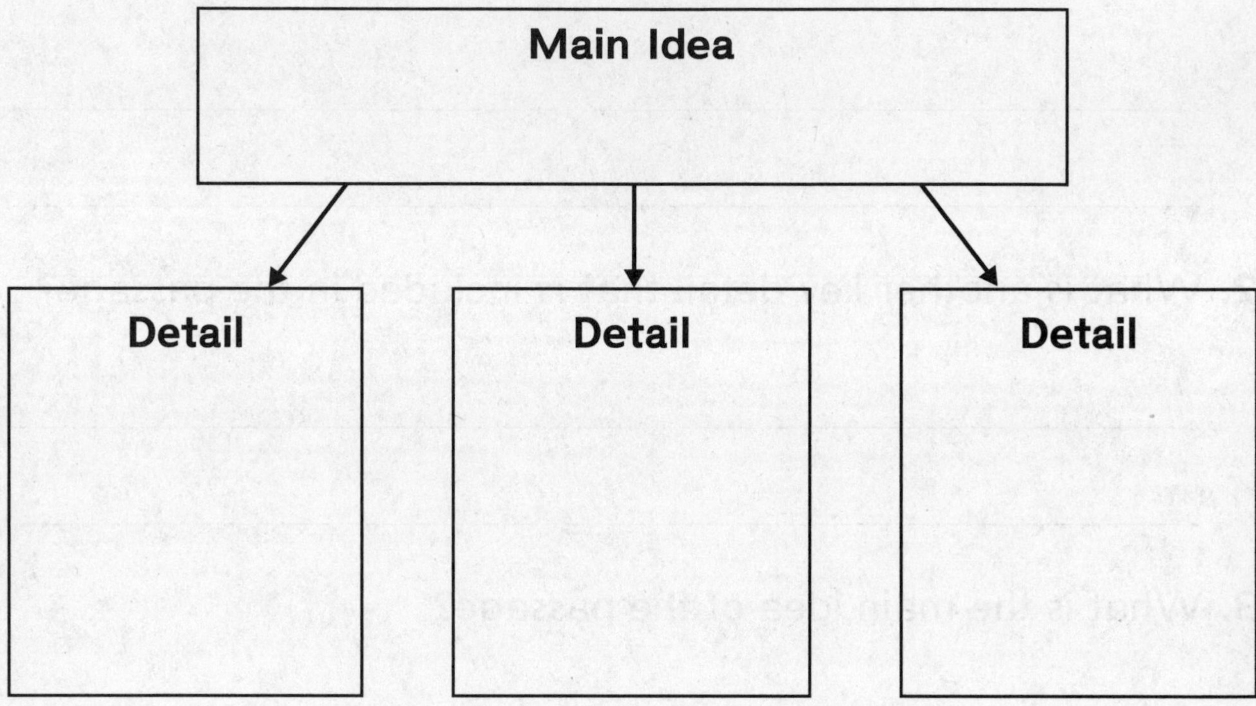

Name ______________________________

Warm Up to Sing

Many singers warm up their voice before they sing. This stretches out their muscles. Humming is one way to warm up. Blowing air through the lips is another way. Singing the musical scales warms up the voice, too.

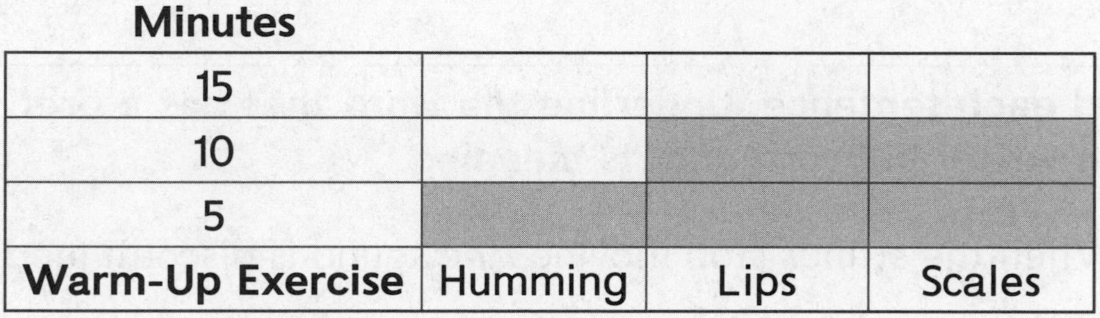

Minutes

15			
10		■	■
5	■	■	■
Warm-Up Exercise	Humming	Lips	Scales

Answer the questions about the text.

1. How do you know this is expository text?

____

____

2. What information can you learn from the bar graph?

____

____

3. How much time do singers spend singing scales?

____

____

Name ______________________________

To figure out a new word, look for a **prefix**, or word part, at the beginning of the word.

The prefix ***re-*** means "again."

The prefix ***un-*** means "not."

The prefix ***dis-*** means "opposite of."

Read each sentence. Underline the word that has a prefix. Then write the word and its meaning.

1. When the strings stop moving, the sound is discontinued.

____

2. You cover and uncover the finger holes using the keys.

____

3. It has an uneven number of valves, three.

____

4. Now let's review the instruments we read about.

____

5. No one can disagree.

____

Name ____

A. Read the draft model. Use the questions that follow the draft to help you think about using sentences of different lengths.

Draft Model

The musician gets her fiddle. She gets ready to play. She tunes up the fiddle. She sets up her sheet music. She plays a lively song.

1. Which sentences could you make longer?

2. Which sentences could you combine?

3. How can you make the sentences flow from one to the next?

B. Now revise the draft by writing sentences of different lengths.

____

____

____

____

____

____

Name ____

Danny used text evidence to answer the prompt: *What different sounds can a person hear at a concert?*

A person can hear many different sounds at a concert. On page 295 of "Many Ways to Enjoy Music," I read that at a concert, there is loud music coming from the stage. People can hear guitars, drums, and other instruments. People can also hear the sounds of people clapping and singing along to the music.

I learned in "A Musical Museum" how people hear these sounds. On page 299, I read that sound is energy that makes things vibrate. When the musicians at the concert play their instruments, they make the instruments vibrate. These vibrations are like waves that make the air vibrate. When the vibrations reach people's ears, they can hear the music.

Reread the passage. Follow the directions below.

1. **Underline** the sentence in which Danny introduces the topic.
2. **Draw a box** around a long sentence and a short sentence that Danny uses.
3. **Circle** a fact about sound that Danny includes.
4. **Write** a sentence on the line in which Danny combined ideas.

____

____.

Name ______________________________

eerie	growth	layers	lively
location	region	seasons	temperate

Choose the word from the box that makes sense in each blank. Then write the word on the line.

1. This high area of the country is the mountain ______________________.
2. A ______________________ of wildflowers fills the meadow.
3. Our class had a ______________________ party at the end of the year.
4. The weather is different in the winter and summer ______________________.
5. The empty house gave us an ______________________ feeling.
6. The gardener digs down through ______________________ of sand and dirt.
7. It is not too hot or cold in a ______________________ climate.
8. Where is the ______________________ of your town on the map?

Name ______________________________

In some letter pairs, one of the letters is silent.

In ***wr***, the ***w*** is silent as in ***wrong***.

In ***kn***, the ***k*** is silent as in ***know***.

In ***gn***, the ***g*** is silent as in ***gnat***.

A. Choose two words from the box that have the same silent letter as each of the words below. Write the words on the line.

wrap	gnu	knife	wrist	knock	gnome

1. write ____________ ____________

2. knot ____________ ____________

3. gnaw ____________ ____________

- The prefix ***re-*** means "again."
- The prefixes ***un-*** and ***dis-*** mean "not" or "opposite of."
- The suffix ***-ful*** means "full of", ***-less*** means "without."

B. Read each word. Write its meaning.

4. playful ____________

5. unsafe ____________

6. resend ____________

7. dishonest ____________

8. sleepless ____________

Name ____

Read the passage. Use the reread strategy to check your understanding of new information or difficult facts.

In a Redwood Forest

A forest is a large area of land covered by trees
11 growing close together. There are different kinds of
19 forests. Some have hardwoods. These forests have trees
27 that lose their leaves each year. Some forests have
36 evergreen trees with needles. One of the most amazing
45 kinds of forests is the redwood forest.

52 What Is a Redwood Tree?

57 In a redwood forest, you will find some of the tallest
68 trees in the world. A redwood tree can grow over
78 300 feet tall. That's as tall as a 35-story skyscraper, a
90 building found in big cities.

95 Redwoods are some of the oldest trees in the world.
105 A redwood tree can live to be 2,000 years old. One
116 reason is these trees can survive fire. Their thick bark
126 keeps them from burning.

Name ______________________________

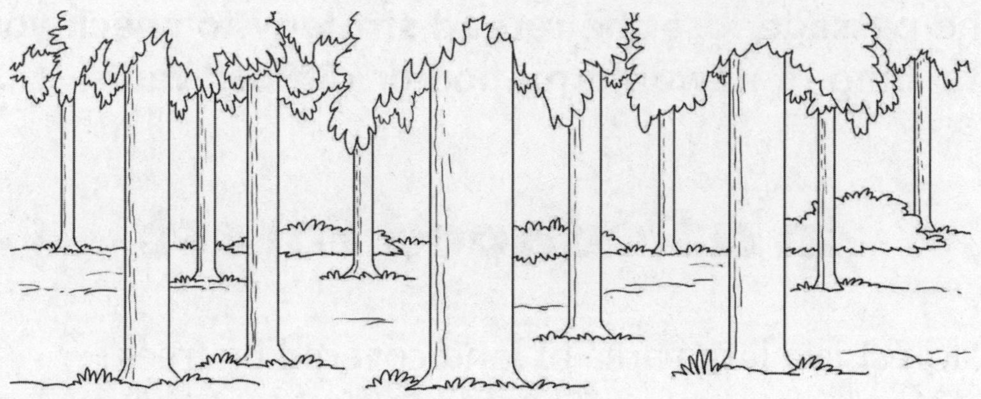

130 **Where Are Redwoods Found?**

134 Redwood forests are not found everywhere. California
141 is the only place where they grow in nature. Redwoods
151 need a wet climate to grow. The coast of California is a
163 good spot.

165 There is fog almost every day. The fog keeps the soil
176 moist. It also helps the redwood trees get water. They
186 soak up water from the fog right into their leaves.

196 In the past, people cut down many redwood trees.
205 These big trees would have disappeared. Now most of
214 them are protected in parks. They can't be destroyed
223 anymore. People can visit the parks to see these special
233 forests.

Name ____________________

A. Reread the passage and answer the questions.

1. How are some forests different from others?

____

____

2. How is a redwood tree like a 35-story skyscraper?

____

____

3. How was the past different for redwood trees than today?

____

____

B. Work with a partner. Read the passage aloud. Pay attention to pronunciation. Stop after one minute. Fill out the chart.

	Words Read	–	Number of Errors	=	Words Correct Score
First Read		–		=	
Second Read		–		=	

Name ____

Read the selection. Complete the Compare and Contrast chart.

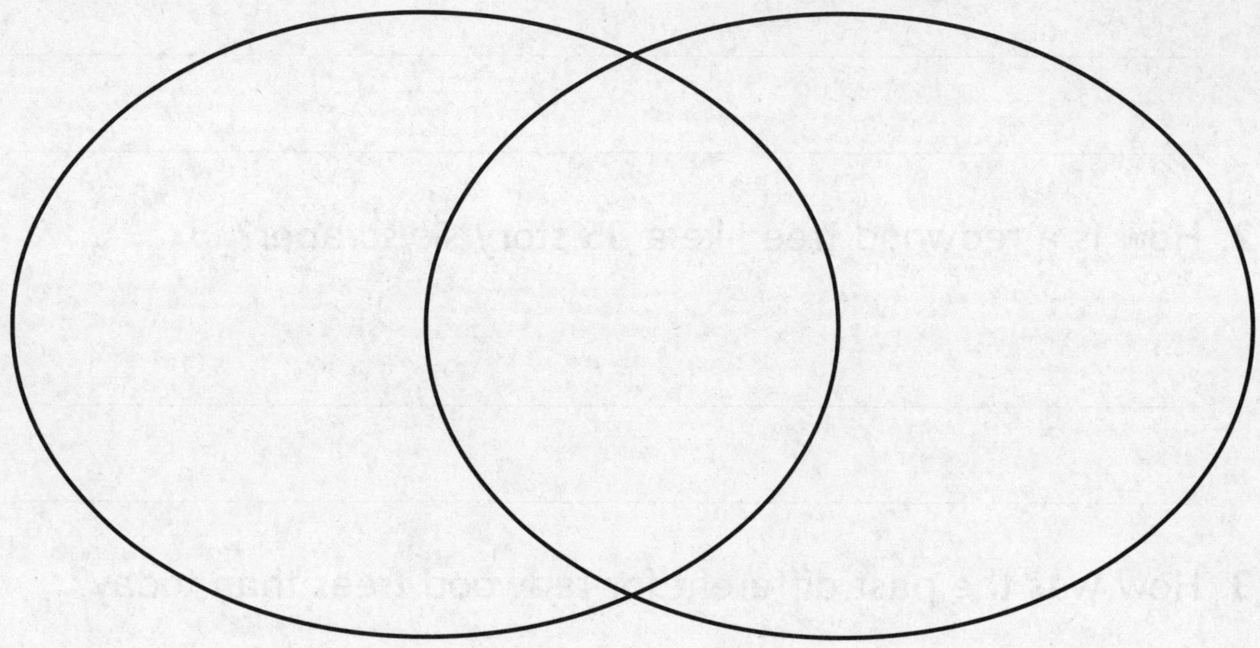

Name ____________________

The Oasis of Mara

The Oasis of Mara is a place with water in the dry Mojave Desert. The water comes from underground. Plants can grow there. Native Americans once lived there.

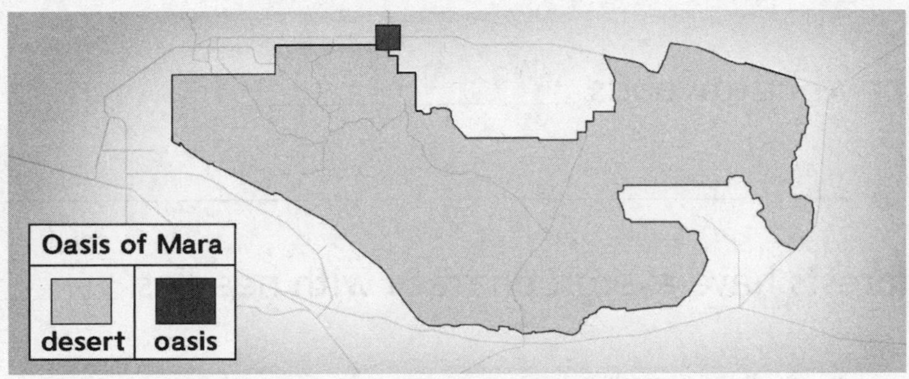

Answer the questions about the text.

1. How do you know this is expository text?

____

____

2. What is the Oasis of Mara?

____

____

3. What does the map show you?

____

____

Name ______________________________

A **compound word** is a word made of two smaller words.

Read each sentence. Write the compound word and draw a line between the two smaller words. Then write the meaning of the compound word.

1. Some have hardwoods. ______________

____

2. Some forests have evergreen trees with needles. ______________

____

3. One of the most amazing kinds of forest is the redwood forest. ______________

____

4. That's as tall as a 35-story skyscraper. ______________

____

5. These forests are not found everywhere. ______________

____

Name ______________________________

A. Read the draft model. Use the questions that follow the draft to help you think about the topic and ideas connected to it.

Draft Model

Some animals here in New Mexico are different from those in Alaska. We don't have moose or caribou, but we do have black bears and elk. The temperature is very hot in the summer. The weather in the winter can be much cooler.

1. What is the topic of the writing?

2. Which ideas connect to the topic?

3. Which ideas do not tell about the topic?

B. Now revise the draft by deleting sentences that do not connect to the topic. Add a new sentence that does connect to the topic.

____

____

____

____

____

____

Name ______________________________

Ángela used text evidence to answer the prompt: *How are rain forests similar to and different from African savannas?*

Rain forests and African savannas are similar and different. They are similar because of where they are on Earth and their temperature. In "Rain Forests," I read that most rain forests grow in hot places near the equator. I learned that African savannas are also very warm, and they are near the equator. Both rain forests and African savannas have many different types of animals and plants.

But rain forests and African savannas are also different. I read that rain forests have many trees and they are close together. African savannas also have trees, but they are spread out. I also learned that rain forests are very wet because it rains there all year long. African savannas only have a few hours of rain each day in the rainy season. Then there may not rain at all in the dry season.

Rain forests and savannas share some of the same features, but they both have unique features too.

Reread the passage. Follow the directions below.

1. Rain forests and savannas are very different places. **Circle** the topic sentence that tells how.

2. **Underline** a fact about rain forests and a fact about savannas.

3. **Draw a box** around the sentence that sums up the answer to the prompt.

4. **Write** an example of a linking verb that Ángela used in the model.

____

Name ____________________

active	earth	explode	island
local	properties	solid	steep

A. Read each clue below. Then find the vocabulary word on the right that matches the clue. Draw a line from the clue to the word.

1. something that is nearby	a. properties
2. land with water all around it	b. active
3. burst loudly with a lot of force	c. steep
4. having a very sharp slope	d. island
5. something that is moving	e. local
6. the traits of something	f. earth
7. the ground or land we walk on	g. solid
8. hard and firm	h. explode

B. Choose one vocabulary word from the box above. Write the word in a sentence of your own.

9. ____________________

____

Name ______________________________

The letters ***er, ir, ur,*** and ***or*** can stand for the same sound. You can hear the sound as you say the words ***fern, third, burn,*** and ***world***.

A. Circle the word that has the vowel sound spelled *er, ir, ur,* or *or*. Write the two letters that make the vowel sound on the line.

1. cuts curve race ____________

2. her rub ring ____________

3. rise worse wrap ____________

4. string wrist first ____________

Before adding *-s, -es, -ed,* or *-ing* to some verbs with short vowels, double the final consonant.

Before adding *-s, -es, -ed,* or *-ing* to some verbs with long vowels ending in *e,* drop the final *e.*

Before adding *-s, -es, -ed,* or *-ing* to some verbs ending in *y,* change *y* to *i.*

B. Write each word with the ending shown.

5. race + ed = ____________ **6.** keep + s = ____________

7. hurry + es = ____________ **8.** trip + ing = ____________

Name ____

Read the passage. Use the reread strategy to check your understanding of new information or difficult facts.

Tsunamis

What Is a Tsunami?

4 You may have seen big **waves** at the beach. Now
14 imagine waves that reach a height of over 100 feet tall!
25 Tsunamis are a set of ocean waves that rush over land.
36 The waves look like giant walls of water.

44 Tsunamis have different **causes**. One event is an
52 undersea earthquake that causes the ocean floor to
60 move and shake. Other causes are underwater landslides
68 or volcanoes. These strong actions build tsunami waves.
76 The waves head for shore, the land along the ocean.

86 When the tsunami waves start, they may be just one
96 foot high. They extend, or reach, deep down into the
106 ocean.

Name ______________________________

107 The waves travel toward shore. The waves can move
116 up to 500 miles per hour. That's as fast as a jet plane.

129 As the waves reach shallow water near land, they slow
139 down. They start to squeeze together. This pushes them
148 higher. Then the big waves hit the shore.

156 **Damage from a Tsunami**

160 Tsunamis cause lots of damage and harm. They can
169 hurt people. They can smash houses and knock down
178 trees. They can cause flooding. They can make drinking
187 water unsafe.

189 **Tsunami Warnings**

191 There are systems in place to warn, or tell, people
201 about tsunamis. People find out the big waves are
210 coming. Then they move to higher ground to stay safe
220 from the tsunamis.

Name ______________________________

A. Reread the passage and answer the questions.

1. What three things can cause a tsunami?

____

____

2. What is the effect when the waves get to shallow water near the land?

____

____

3. What happens when people get a tsunami warning?

____

____

B. Work with a partner. Read the passage aloud. Pay attention to where you pause and how you group words together. Stop after one minute. Fill out the chart.

	Words Read	–	Number of Errors	=	Words Correct Score
First Read		–		=	
Second Read		–		=	

Name ____

Read the selection. Complete the Cause and Effect chart.

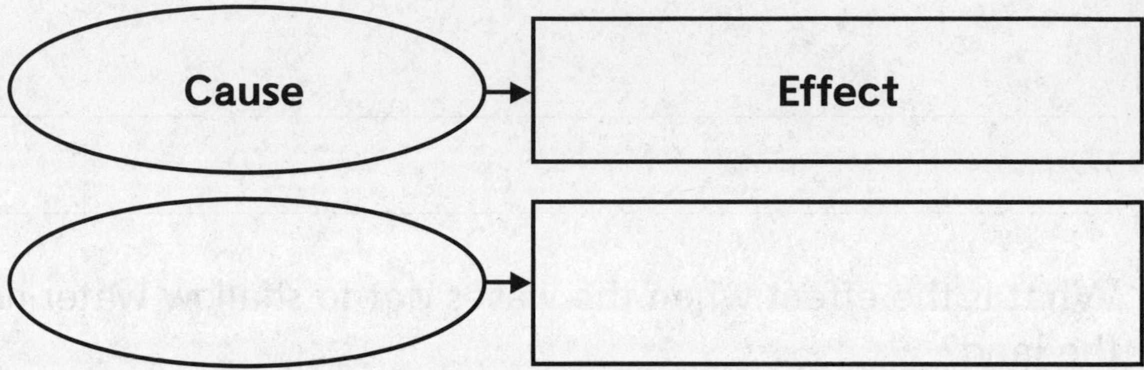

Name ________________________________

Avalanche

An **avalanche** is a snow slide. High on a mountain, a big **chunk** of snow breaks loose. This snow slides down the **slope**, moving fast. It piles up at the bottom of the mountain.

Answer the questions about the text.

1. How do you know this is expository text?

____

____

2. Why are the words **avalanche, chunk,** and **slope** in bold print?

____

3. What is the cause of an avalanche?

____

4. What is the effect of an avalanche?

____

____

Name ____

Look at this example of **context clues** in a sentence. The underlined words explain what *height* means.

Now imagine waves that reach a **height** of over <u>100 feet tall</u>!

Read each sentence. Write the meaning of the word in bold print. Underline the context clues in the sentence that helped you.

1. **Tsunamis** are a set of ocean waves that rush over land.

____

2. One event is an undersea **earthquake** that causes the ocean floor to move and shake.

____

3. They **extend**, or reach, deep down into the ocean.

____

4. The waves head for **shore**, the land along the ocean.

____

5. Tsunamis cause lots of **damage** and harm.

____

Name ____________________

A. Read the draft model. Use the questions that follow the draft to help you add time-order words.

Draft Model

Some beaches have steep cliffs of rock. Waves crash into the rock. Tiny pieces of rock wash away. The top of the cliff can fall into the sea.

1. What happens first in the process of beach erosion, or washing away? What happens next?

2. What event happens last?

3. What time-order words can you add to make the order of events more clear?

B. Now revise the draft by adding time-order words such as *first, next, after,* and *last* to help readers understand the order of events.

____

____

____

____

____

____

Name ______________________________

Madison used text evidence to answer the prompt: *Why are volcanoes and wildfires proof that Earth is always changing?*

Volcanoes and wildfires both cause Earth to change. They are proof that Earth is always changing.

I read on pages 325 and 326 of "Volcanoes" that lava has formed mountains and islands as it spread out on Earth's surface and cooled. Lava has destroyed entire forests because it is so hot. It has burned some forests to the ground. On page 331, I read that the ash from volcanoes has helped some plants grow.

In "To the Rescue," I read on page 334 that wildfires burn trees and plants. This happens right away. Later, new plants may grow back where the wildfire happened.

Volcanoes and wildfires prove that Earth is always changing.

Reread the passage. Follow the directions below.

1. **Draw a box** around the sentence that introduces the topic.
2. **Underline** the text evidence that tells how lava can reshape Earth.
3. **Circle** a time-order word that Madison uses to tell when plants grow back after a wildfire.
4. **On** the line, write an example of a helping verb.

____

Name ____

common	costume	customs	favorite
parades	surrounded	travels	wonder

Read the story. Choose words from the box to complete the sentences. Then write the answers on the lines.

My family ____________________ around the country. We see different ____________________ and celebrations wherever we go.

We visited a town that is ____________________ by farms. In summer the people gather in a shared space, or ____________________ area for a harvest fair.

We also visited a city that has many ____________________ in the streets. The marching clowns are my ____________________ part. Each clown wears a funny ____________________.

I ____________________ what we will see next!

Name ______________________________

The letters ***or, ore,*** and ***oar*** can make the same sound. You can hear the sound in the words ***short, chore,*** and ***soar***.

The letters ***ar*** can stand for the sound you hear in the word ***arm***.

A. Read the words in the box. Circle the letters that stand for the vowel sound. Then write each word below the picture with the same vowel sound.

park   roar   scarf   yard   score   north

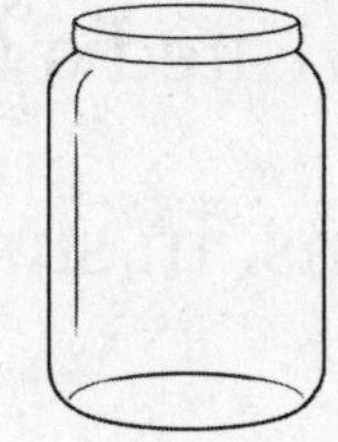

1. ______________________ 4. ______________________

2. ______________________ 5. ______________________

3. ______________________ 6. ______________________

Some nouns change their spelling to name more than one, as in ***man*** and ***men***.

B. Write the plural form for each word.

7. tooth ______________ 8. child ______________

Name ______________________________

Read the passage. Use the visualize strategy to form pictures in your mind about what happens in the story.

Giving Thanks Two Times

It was a cool November day. The dim sun hung like
11 a nickel in the sky. My friend Riku and I were walking
23 home from school. I hugged my arms when I felt
33 a breeze as sharp as a knife.

40 That day at school, we had studied Thanksgiving.
48 We learned that the early settlers celebrated their first
57 harvest at this very time of year. They had a big feast to
70 give thanks for all they had.

76 "My dad bought a turkey as big as a pillow. Are you
88 having a big turkey for Thanksgiving?" I asked Riku.

97 He grinned wide as he answered. "Yes, we're having a
107 turkey. And we're having rice, too!"

Name ____

113 Riku explained that his family was celebrating Labor
121 Day Thanksgiving. It was a holiday in Japan, where
130 his family had lived. He told me that this holiday was a
142 harvest celebration, just like American Thanksgiving.

148 "Both holidays are in November, too!" I exclaimed.

156 Riku told me that last year he missed American
165 Thanksgiving. He had spent Labor Day Thanksgiving
172 in Japan. He was visiting his grandparents. He saw
181 parades. There were displays of fruits and vegetables,
189 like colorful rainbows.

192 "That was to give thanks for good crops," explained
201 Riku.

202 "You're lucky," I said. "You get to have two
211 Thanksgivings."

212 Riku said, "Why don't you visit my family for
221 Labor Day Thanksgiving? Then you can have two
229 Thanksgivings also!"

Name ____________________

A. Reread the passage and answer the questions.

1. How are Thanksgiving and Labor Day Thanksgiving alike?

____

____

2. How are Thanksgiving and Labor Day Thanksgiving different?

____

____

3. How do the narrator and Riku celebrate their holidays in the same way?

____

____

B. Work with a partner. Read the passage aloud. Pay attention to how you use your voice to show feelings. Stop after one minute. Fill out the chart.

	Words Read	–	Number of Errors	=	Words Correct Score
First Read		–		=	
Second Read		–		=	

Name ____

Read the selection. Complete the Compare and Contrast chart.

Name ______________________________

Going to School

My name is Alba. I go to school in Mexico. I study six subjects, including Spanish and English. At lunchtime, I buy food at the school store and eat outside with my friends.

Answer the questions about the text.

1. How can you tell that this is realistic fiction?

____

____

2. Who is telling the story? How do you know?

____

____

3. What is one realistic event that Alba tells about?

____

____

Name ______________________________

A **simile** compares two unlike things. It uses the word *like* or *as* to make the comparison.

Read the sentences. Then answer the questions.

1. The dim sun hung like a nickel in the sky.

   What two things does the author compare? ____________

   ____

   What does the simile mean? ____________

   ____

2. My dad bought a turkey as big as a pillow.

   What two things does the author compare? ____________

   ____

   What does the simile mean? ____________

   ____

3. There were displays of fruits and vegetables, like colorful rainbows.

   What two things does the author compare? ____________

   ____

   What does the simile mean? ____________

   ____

Name ______________________________

A. Read the draft model. Use the questions that follow the draft to help you add words, descriptions, and punctuation to show the writer's feelings.

Draft Model

Dear Frank,

Last week I went to a Cinco de Mayo celebration. There was music and dancing. Bands played Mexican music. People wore costumes. There was even Mexican food.

Your friend,

Maxine

1. How does the writer feel about the celebration?

2. What words might describe the music, dancing, and costumes?

3. Where can you add punctuation to show how the writer feels?

B. Revise the draft by adding words, descriptions, and punctuation to show how the writer feels about the Cinco de Mayo celebration.

____

____

____

____

Name ____

Kevin used text evidence to answer the prompt: *Write a letter from Carlitos to Charlie about a new game he learned called Snail.*

Dear Primo Charlie,

Today I learned a new game called *Snail.* I think you'll like it.

I remember you told me that you play games with your friends after school. You can play this game anywhere. All you need is some concrete and chalk.

Anyway, *Snail* is a lot like hopscotch. First, you draw a big snail with numbers in the shell on the ground. Then you try to hop to the center on one foot. You take turns with your friends. If you put two feet down, you lose a turn.

I played *Snail* at school, but tomorrow is Saturday and I will be at home. I'm going to draw the snail in the dirt with a stick.
I want to play it with my little sister. It's going to be so much fun!
I can't wait to see you! You had better practice!

Your friend,
Carlitos

Reread the passage. Follow the directions below.

1. **Circle** an event that tells Carlitos's thoughts about the game.

2. **Draw a box** around two words that show the order of the game.

3. **Underline** a sentence that shows Carlitos's voice.

4. **Write** an example of an irregular verb.

____

Name ______________________________

ashamed	boast	dash	holler
plenty	similarities	victory	wisdom

Write the word on the line that makes sense.

1. There are ______________________ of books to read at the library.

2. The girl had to ______________________ to class when the bell rang.

3. The team is proud of their ______________________ in the game.

4. Can you name the ______________________ between a frog and a toad?

5. The man used his ______________________ to make the right choice.

6. The student felt ______________________ about not telling the truth.

7. The fans ______________________ loudly at the game.

8. She likes to ______________________ about her smart puppy.

Name ____________________

The letters ***eer, ere,*** and ***ear*** can stand for the **same** sound. Listen to the sound as you say the words ***steer, here,*** and ***clear***.

A. Read each word. Circle the words that rhyme with the first word.

1. **year** fern mere spear jeer
2. **peer** perk cheer near fear
3. **here** dear herd veer ear

An abbreviation is a short way to write a word. It begins with a capital letter and ends with a period.

B. Read each sentence. Write the underlined name on the line, using the correct abbreviation.

1. Mister Flint is a teacher. ____________
2. The school is on North Street. ____________
3. My friend lives on Turner Avenue. ____________
4. Doctor Lopez cares for pets. ____________

Name ____

Read the passage. Use the visualize strategy to form pictures in your mind about what happens in the play.

Coyote Brings Fire

Characters		
Narrator	Coyote	Squirrel
Chipmunk	Frog	Two Fire Beings

Narrator: Long ago, people did not have fire. Coyote
9 decided to bring it to them.

15 (Coyote speaks to Squirrel, Chipmunk, and Frog.)

22 **Coyote:** I know where we can get fire. The Fire Beings
33 have it at their camp. I have a workable plan to take the
46 fire. Will you help?

50 **Squirrel:** We'll all help you if you just tell us what to do.

63 **Coyote:** Follow me very quietly.

68 (The animals sneak up to the Fire Beings' camp. Coyote
78 grabs a stick of fire and runs.)

85 **Chipmunk:** Look out, Coyote! The Fire Beings are
93 chasing you. Run quickly!

97 **Frog:** The Fire Beings touched the end of Coyote's tail!
107 Now the fur there is white.

Name ____

113 **Squirrel:** Coyote, toss the fire to me and I'll catch it.

124 (Coyote tosses the fire to Squirrel.)

130 **Coyote:** Oh, Squirrel, you caught the fire with your
139 tail. The heat of the fire has curled your tail up over
151 your back.

153 **Chipmunk:** Squirrel, toss the fire here to me.

161 (Squirrel tosses the fire to Chipmunk.)

167 **Coyote:** Watch out, Chipmunk, a Fire Being is right
176 behind you.

178 **Frog:** The Fire Being scratched Chipmunk's back. Look
186 at the three stripes on his back. Throw the fire to me,
198 Chipmunk!

199 (Chipmunk tosses the fire to Frog. Frog is caught by a Fire
211 Being, but gets away. The fire being still holds Frog's tail.)

222 **Squirrel:** Frog, you have lost your tail!

229 **Coyote:** Here comes another Fire Being. Frog, toss the
238 fire onto Wood.

241 **Narrator:** Now Wood had fire. Coyote showed the
249 people a useful skill. He rubbed two sticks together to
259 make fire. From that day on, the people had fire.

Name ____

A. Reread the passage and answer the questions.

1. What does Coyote want to do for people?

____

____

2. How do Coyote and the animals get fire?

____

____

3. What is the theme of the passage?

____

____

B. Work with a partner. Read the passage aloud. Pay attention to how you use your voice to show feelings. Stop after one minute. Fill out the chart.

	Words Read	–	Number of Errors	=	Words Correct Score
First Read		–		=	
Second Read		–		=	

Name ____

Read the selection. Complete the Theme chart.

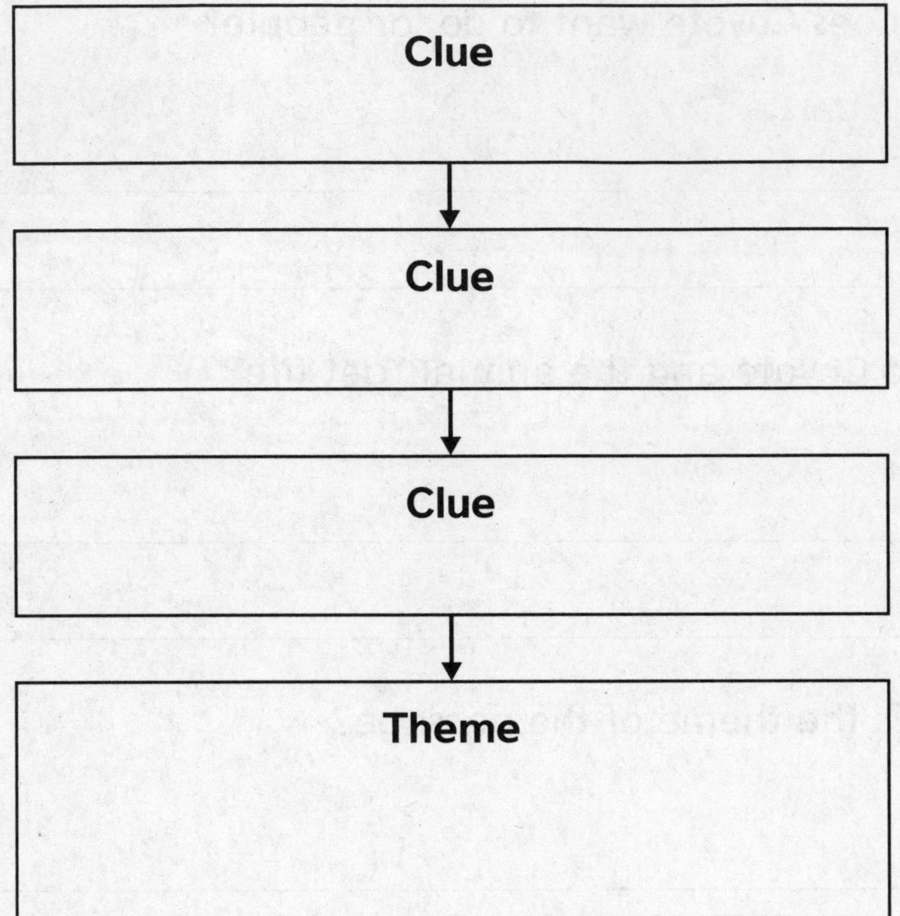

Name ______________________________

Bear's Stumpy Tail

Fox: Bear, drop your tail in this hole in the ice. You can catch fish that way.

(Bear sits to put his tail in the ice.)

Bear: My tail is cold. I'm getting up now.

(Bear gets up. His tail snaps off. Now he has a stumpy tail.)

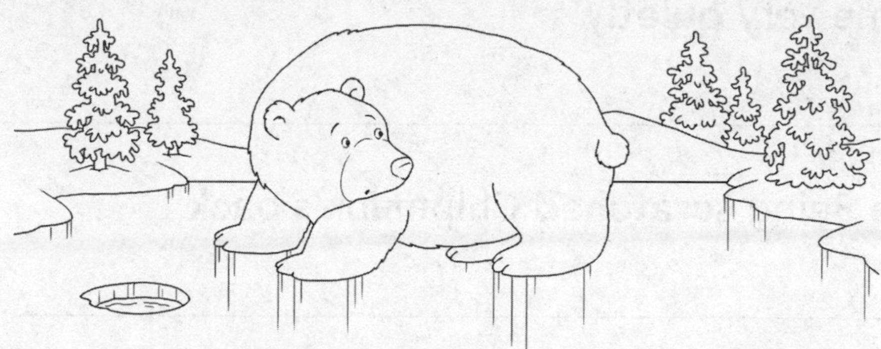

Answer the questions about the text.

1. How do you know this is a drama?

____

____

2. Why does Bear drop his tail into the hole in the ice?

____

3. What lesson does Bear learn about Fox?

____

Name ______________________________

A **root word** is a word to which other word parts are added.

Read each sentence. Circle the root word in the word in bold print. Then write the meaning of the word in bold print.

1. I have a **workable** plan to take the fire.

____

2. Follow me very **quietly**.

____

3. The Fire Being **scratched** Chipmunk's back.

____

4. The Fire Being still **holds** Frog's tail.

____

5. Coyote showed the people a **useful** skill.

____

Name ________________________________

A. Read the draft model. Use the questions that follow the draft to help you add details about the characters' experiences and thoughts.

Draft Model

Sun and Moon were friends. They were nice to each other. Every day they had fun and did things together.

1. What might Sun and Moon think about being friends?
2. How might Sun and Moon be nice to each other?
3. What kind of fun might they have together? What are some things they might do?

B. Now revise the draft by adding details that tell about what Sun and Moon are like.

____

____

____

____

____

____

____

Name ____

Lily used text evidence to answer the prompt: *If you were one of the birds from "How the Finch Got its Colors," which design do you think you would choose if you won the race?*

If I were one of the birds from "How the Finch Got Its Colors," I would choose a colorful design with dots and circles. In the folktale about the Finch, the birds quickly began fighting over the colors. The hummingbird wanted the very best colors for herself. She chose bright, beautiful colors of "purple, green, and black." Those colors would look fantastic when I am flying through the blue sky and the white clouds. Those are the colors I would choose.

In "How the Beetle Got Her Colors," Agouti describes "shiny designs" on Arrow Frog's skin. The designs are very unique. They would make my feathers looks very special. No one would confuse me with anyone other animal. So, bright colorful feathers with a shiny design on them would be my prize for winning the race.

Reread the passage. Follow the directions below.

1. **Circle** a detail from the story that tells about hummingbird's character.

2. **Draw a box** around a detail from the story that supports Lily's opinion.

3. **Underline** the conclusion that sums up Lily's response.

4. **Write** one of the irregular verbs that Lily uses on the line.

____

Name ______________________________

drops	excite	outdoors	pale

A. Choose the word that makes sense for each clue. Write the word on the line.

1. to give a strong feeling of enjoyment ______________

2. not inside a building ______________

3. very light in color ______________

4. small amounts of liquid ______________

B. Complete each sentence with a word from the box above.

5. We play ______________ when the weather is nice.

6. I spilled some ______________ of paint on the floor.

7. The sky was ______________ blue in the early morning.

8. Squirrels playing outside the window will ______________ our cat for hours.

C. Choose one vocabulary word from the box above. Write the word in a sentence of your own.

9. ____

Name ______________________________

The letters ***are, air, ear,*** and ***ere*** can stand for the vowel sound you hear in ***air***.

A. Read each row of words. Circle the word that has the same vowel sound as in *care*. Write the word on the line. Then underline the letters that spell the vowel sound.

1. peek paint pear ______________
2. where wheel when ______________
3. date dare dance ______________
4. chore chair chase ______________
5. hair here hard ______________
6. bark bean bear ______________

When a vowel or a pair of vowels is followed by the letter ***r***, it changes the vowel sound. The vowels and the ***r*** stay in the same syllable.

B. Read each word. Draw a line between the syllables.

7. haircut
8. airport
9. turkey
10. perfect

Name ________________________________

Read the poem. Use the visualize strategy to form pictures in your mind about what happens in the poem.

The First Skate

The temperature has been below freezing for days.
08 The pond is frozen now,
13 The ice is as smooth as glass.
20 I can ice skate outdoors
25 For the first time this winter.
31 I put on my skates and lace them up tight.
41 Then I step onto the ice and push off.
50 Right foot, left foot, right foot, left foot,
58 I glide over the ice like a bird.
66 I spin in a circle and start over again.

Name ____

75 I look up,
78 Overhead, the sky curves like a blue bowl.
86 I look down,
89 Below the ice, frozen bubbles look like crystal beads.
98 As I skate, the cool breeze feels like cold fingers on my face,
111 My cheeks turn as red as apples.
118 I'm warm inside, though,
122 It feels like a fire glowing,
128 As I skate round and round the pond.
136 I keep telling myself, "One more time,"
143 Until at last it is the last time and I step off the ice,
157 Land-bound once again.

Name ____________________

A. Reread the passage and answer the questions.

1. What was the setting of the poem?

____

____

2. What did the girl do?

____

____

3. What is the theme of the poem?

____

____

B. Work with a partner. Read the passage aloud. Pay attention to how you pause and group words together. Stop after one minute. Fill out the chart.

	Words Read	–	Number of Errors	=	Words Correct Score
First Read		–		=	
Second Read		–		=	

Name ____

Read the selection. Complete the Theme chart.

Clue

↓

Clue

↓

Clue

↓

Theme

Name ____

A Rainy Day

The rain is pouring, pouring down,
It's so boring to stay inside.
The rain is dripping, dripping slowly.
Is it going to rain all day?
The rain is stopping, stopping now.
I can go outside and have some fun!

Answer the questions about the text.

1. How do you know this text is a poem?

____

2. What words does the poet repeat in the poem?

____

3. Why do you think the poet uses repetition?

____

Name ____

A **simile** compares two different things using the word ***like*** or ***as***.

Read the lines from the poem. Answer the questions. Then explain what each simile means.

1. The ice is as smooth as glass.

   What two things does the author compare?

   ____

   Meaning: ____

2. Overhead, the sky curves like a blue bowl.

   What two things does the author compare?

   ____

   Meaning: ____

3. Below the ice, frozen bubbles look like crystal beads.

   What two things does the author compare?

   ____

   Meaning: ____

4. My cheeks turn as red as apples.

   What two things does the author compare?

   ____

   Meaning: ____

Name ______________________________

A. Read the draft model. Use the questions that follow the draft to help you think about what sensory words you can add.

Draft Model

A butterfly flies by.
Its wings are like bright jewels.
It stops at a flower.

1. How does the butterfly move?

2. How do its wings look?

3. What does the flower look like? How does it smell?

B. Now revise the draft by adding sensory words about the butterfly and the flower.

____

____

____

____

____

Name ____

Ryan used text evidence to answer the prompt: *In your opinion, which poem, "Rain Poem" or "Windy Tree," best helps you to picture what the poem is talking about?*

The poem "Windy Tree" gives me the clearest picture. I read that the tree's trunk is very strong. It's like a leg with many muscles. It holds on with its foot and "its wide-spread toes" while the wind blows hard. These words help me visualize the tree. I can see its strong branches and feel the rough bark of the tree trunk. I understand how strong it is.

The author of "Rain Song" compares the rain to a little gray mouse. She says that the rain found an open window and "left tracks across the sill." I can picture a furry gray mouse, and I know how shy some mice are. I think the rain is not a storm, but gentle drops. However, the description the author uses in "Windy Tree" gives me a clearer picture of the strong tree blowing in the wind than the description of the rain falling in "Rain Song."

Reread the passage. Follow the directions below.

1. The weather is very different in these poems. **Underline** a detail that supports the child's opinion.
2. **Draw a box** around the text evidence that helps you describe what you see in your mind.
3. **Circle** the text evidence that sums up Ryan's opinion.
4. **Write** an example of a contraction that is used in the model.

____

Name ____

champion	determined	issues	promises
responsibility	rights	volunteered	votes

A. Choose the word that makes sense for each clue. Write the word on the line.

1. offered to do something ______________
2. important things that people are talking about ____________
3. choices given by people to elect someone ______________
4. decided on something ______________
5. a duty to do something ______________
6. things you say you will do ______________
7. a person who has won a contest ______________
8. the things the law says you can do or have ______________

B. Choose one vocabulary word from the box above. Write the word in a sentence of your own.

9. ____

____

____

Name ____________________

Two letters blended together can stand for one vowel sound. The letters ***ou*** and ***ow*** can stand for the vowel sound in ***south*** and ***down***.

A. Read the words. Circle the word that has a different vowel sound. Write the word on the line and circle the letters that spell the vowel sound.

1. cloud you group ____________

2. blue round fruit ____________

3. slow throw cow ____________

4. pull shout push ____________

5. crown snow road ____________

Some nouns have special plural forms. They change their spelling to name more than one.

B. Write the plural form for each word.

6. mouse ____________ **7.** child ____________

8. foot ____________ **9.** man ____________

Name ____

Read the passage. Use the summarize strategy to tell the important events in your own words.

The Lost Kitten

00 One day, my friend Cora and I saw a homemade
10 sign posted on our street. The sign had a photo of a
22 kitten and the words, *LOST KITTEN. Please call Sally*
31 *at 555-0505 if you find my kitten, Boots.*

38 "Sally is our neighbor, Pam. She just got a new kitten
49 and now her pet is missing. It's too bad there's nothing
60 we can do," Cora said sadly.

66 I spoke up. "It's not hopeless. There is something
75 we can do! We can ask our neighbors to help look for
87 Boots."

88 We asked my dad to help with our neighborhood
97 search plan. First, we went and talked to Sally.

106 Sally explained what had happened, "I was careless
114 enough to leave the back door open. Boots slipped out
124 and ran off. And I haven't seen him since."

133 "Don't worry," I said. "We have a plan to help. Come
144 with us."

Name ______________________________

146 We all went to Mrs. Lowe's house. After Mrs. Lowe
156 heard our plan, she said, "I think that's a wonderful
166 idea. It's very thoughtful of you to help Sally find Boots.
177 I'll be happy to help with the search." She joined our
188 group.

189 At each house on the street, the answer was the same.
200 Each neighbor would gladly help search for Boots. Dad
209 divided up the neighborhood streets and told each group
218 where to look.

221 Cora and I were calling loudly, "Boots!" Suddenly we
230 heard a soft mewing sound near our feet. There was
240 Boots, crouching under a bush. I held out my hand and
251 softly called Boots's name. He came right to me and I
262 scooped up the tiny kitten.

267 When we returned Boots to Sally, she was very
276 thankful. She hugged her kitten tightly as she said,
285 "The neighborhood search plan worked. Thank you,
292 everyone!"

Name ______________________________

A. Reread the passage and answer the questions.

1. How does Cora feel about the missing kitten?

____

____

2. What clues help you understand Cora's point of view?

____

____

3. At the end of the story, what clues help you understand Sally's point of view?

____

____

B. Work with a partner. Read the passage aloud. Pay attention to how you raise and lower your voice. Stop after one minute. Fill out the chart.

	Words Read	–	Number of Errors	=	Words Correct Score
First Read		–		=	
Second Read		–		=	

Name ________________________________

Read the selection.
Complete the Point of View chart.

Character	Clue	Point of View

Name ______________________________

Reading Volunteers

My name is Derek. The children in my second-grade class know how to read. Every Friday, we visit Ms. Snow's first-grade class. I pair up with Jack and help him practice reading. It feels good to help others.

Answer the questions about the text.

1. How can you tell that this text is realistic fiction?

____

____

2. Who is telling the story? How do you know?

____

____

3. How does Derek feel about helping Jack learn to read? Why do you think so?

____

____

Name ____

To figure out a new word, look for a **suffix**, or word part, added to the end of the word.

The suffix ***-ly*** means "in a way that is."

The suffix ***-ful*** means "full of."

The suffix ***-less*** means "without."

A. Underline the suffix in the word in bold print. Then write the word and its meaning.

1. "It's too bad there's nothing we can do," Cora said **sadly**.

____

2. I was **careless** enough to leave the back door open.

____

3. It's very **thoughtful** of you to help Sally find Boots.

____

B. Write a word that means the same as the group of words. Your new word will end in *-ful* or *-less*.

4. without thought

____

5. full of thanks

____

Name ____________________

A. Read the draft model. Use the questions that follow the draft to help you think about descriptive details you can add.

Draft Model

Our class helped at the park. We planted a lot of things. I used a shovel to dig holes for trees. Other kids helped, too. The park looked great at the end of the day.

1. What kind of class is helping in the park?

2. What does the park look like?

3. What details might describe the kinds of things the class planted? What details might tell how the park looks at the end of the day?

B. Now revise the draft by adding descriptive details that help readers learn more about the characters, setting, and events.

Name ______________________________

Jordan used text evidence to answer the prompt: ***In your opinion, are Grace and Matthew responsible members of their communities?***

I think Grace and Matthew are both responsible members of their communities. Grace listens to the issues that are important to other students. She makes promises to make her school a better place, like making bullying and littering against the rules. She even keeps some of her promises before she is elected. Grace organized a beautification committee, volunteered in the school cafeteria, and joined the safety squad. She does a lot of hard work for her community without being asked.

Matthew also helps other kids. He feels lucky that he is able to go to Camp Smiles. He thinks other kids with disabilities should have the same opportunity. Like Grace, he is involved in his community. He asks for help to raise money for kids who can't afford to go to Camp Smiles. He helps make other kids smile! This is why Grace and Matthew are both responsible members of their communities. They are good citizens.

Reread the passage. Follow the directions below.

1. **Circle** the topic sentence.

2. **Draw a box** around a detail that tells how Matthew is a responsible member of his community.

3. **Underline** the conclusion.

4. **Write** a plural pronoun Jordan used on the line.

____

Name ______________________________

amused	cooperate	describe	entertained
imagination	interact	patient	peaceful

Choose the word that makes sense in each blank. Then write the word on the line.

1. The book club members talk and ______________ with each other when they meet.

2. The singers ______________ the people at the show.

3. My friend ______________ us with his funny jokes.

4. The firefighters work together, or ______________, to put out the fire.

5. When there is a long line at lunch, you must be ______________.

6. It is easy to relax in a ______________ place.

7. Can you ______________ the drawing you made?

8. You can write a good story when you use your ______________.

Name ____

Two letters blended together can stand for one vowel sound. The letters ***oy*** and ***oi*** can stand for the vowel sound in ***boy*** and ***foil***.

A. Read each sentence. Circle the word with the vowel sound you hear in *boy*. Write the word on the line and circle the letters that spell the vowel sound.

1. The girl plays with a toy truck. ______________
2. We'll plant seeds in the soil and watch them grow. ___________
3. Dad will boil eggs in a pot on the stove. ______________
4. The baby giggles with joy when she is tickled. ____________

When a word ends in ***-le,*** the consonant before it plus the letters ***le*** form the last syllable. This sound in an end syllable can also be spelled ***-al*** or ***-el***.

B. Read each word. Draw a line between the syllables. Write each syllable on the line.

1. needle ______________ ______________
2. bagel ______________ ______________
3. local ______________ ______________
4. puzzle ______________ ______________

Name ______________________________

Read the passage. Use the summarize strategy to tell the important events in your own words.

The Class Play

00 Mr. Webb's class was going to put on a play for the
12 school. They chose to act out *Henny Penny.*

20 "There are six actors in this play," said Mr. Webb.
30 "We'll need painters for the sets. We'll need helpers with
40 the lights and music. There will be a job for everyone."

51 The next day, the class read the play together. Luz
61 said, "I'm going to play the part of Henny Penny. That's
72 the most important part."

76 "No, I want to play that part," said Jade.

85 "I think I would be the best Henny Penny," chimed in
96 Stacy.

97 Before the talk could get out of hand, Mr. Webb spoke
108 up. "We have to be fair. We will have a try-out and I
122 will be the judge."

Name ______________________________________

126 Mr. Webb explained that children who wanted to act
135 in the play should practice the lines. Then Mr. Webb
145 would decide who was best for each part.

153 The class agreed that this was fair. They knew if they
164 all pulled together, they could put on a great play.

174 Luz made up her mind that she wanted to play Henny
185 Penny. She practiced her lines over and over. She knew
195 the lines by heart.

199 At the try-out, three children read the part of Henny
210 Penny. Other children tried out for the rest of the parts.
221 Mr. Webb clapped for each child. Then he said, "Luz,
231 you will play Henny Penny. Here is a list of the other
243 parts and jobs for all."

248 The class worked hard on their play. Everyone at
257 school said it was a big hit!

Name ____

A. Reread the passage and answer the questions.

1. What is Luz's point of view about who should play the part of Henny Penny?

____

____

2. What is Stacy's point of view about who should play the part of Henny Penny?

____

____

3. What is Mr. Webb's point of view about who should play the part of Henny Penny?

____

____

B. Work with a partner. Read the passage aloud. Pay attention to how you use your voice to show feelings. Stop after one minute. Fill out the chart.

	Words Read	–	Number of Errors	=	Words Correct Score
First Read		–		=	
Second Read		–		=	

Name ______________________________

Read the selection.
Complete the Point of View chart.

Character	Clue	Point of View

Name ______________________________

Sharing the Class Pet

Marta's class has a pet rabbit. On Friday, everyone wants to take the rabbit home. Mrs. Jones writes the children's names on papers and mixes them up. She will pick a name to see who takes the rabbit home today.

Answer the questions about the text.

1. How do you know that this text is fiction?

____

____

2. What is the problem?

____

____

3. What is the solution?

____

____

Name ______________________________

An **idiom** is a word or a phrase that has a different meaning than the real meaning of the words.

Read each sentence. Look at the idiom in bold print. Write the meaning of the idiom.

1. Before the talk could **get out of hand**, Mr. Webb spoke up.

____

2. They knew if they all **pulled together**, they could put on a great play.

____

3. Luz **made up her mind** that she wanted to play Henny Penny.

____

4. She **knew the lines by heart**.

____

5. Everyone at school said **it was a big hit**!

____

Name ____

A. Read the draft model. Use the questions that follow the draft to help you think about using sentences of different lengths.

Draft Model

Jake had to do a project. It was for science. He and his friends worked together. It made the work go faster. They built a toy rocket ship. Soon they were done.

1. Which sentences could you make longer?

2. Which sentences could you combine?

3. How can you make the sentences flow from one to the next?

B. Now revise the draft by writing sentences of different lengths.

____

____

____

____

____

____

____

Name ______________________________

Rachel used text evidence to answer the prompt: *In your opinion, what are the benefits of cooperating with others?*

I think that there any many benefits of cooperating with others, but there are two that I think are very important. Cooperating with others makes people happier. It also makes communities safer.

At the beginning of *Once Upon a Baby Brother,* Lizzie couldn't wait to go to school each morning so that she could get away from her brother, Marvin. At the end, she learned how to cooperate with him. She used him as a character in her comic book. She read the story to Marvin and she even hugged him. In the illustrations, I can see she looks much happier.

In "Bully-Free Zone," students in Seattle worked together to stop bullying. They learned how to be good friends to each other. After this, students didn't pick on each other very much. The students cooperated and the schools in Seattle were safer for everybody.

I think cooperating with others is always a good idea!

Reread the passage. Follow the directions below.

1. **Circle** Rachel's topic sentence.
2. **Draw a box** around two linking words.
3. **Underline** one short sentence and one long sentence.
4. **Write** a sentence with the pronoun *I* on the line.

____

____

Name ______________________________

agree	challenging	discover	heroes
interest	perform	succeed	study

Choose the word that makes sense in each blank. Then write the word on the line.

1. My aunt has an ______________ in learning to knit.
2. The boy found it ______________ to complete the puzzle.
3. Do you ______________ or disagree with my idea?
4. You should ______________ the spelling words before taking the test.
5. The ______________ helped many people to safety.
6. I would like to ______________ a new star in the sky.
7. Five actors ______________ in a play on stage.
8. You can ______________ at playing the piano with lots of practice.

Name ______________________________

The letters ***oo, u_e, u, ew, ue,*** and ***ui*** can stand for the vowel sound you hear in the words ***moon, tune, flu, chew, blue,*** and ***suit***. The letters ***oo, ou,*** and ***u*** can also stand for the vowel sound you hear in **look, would,** and **push**.

A. Write each word in the box to match the word in bold print with the same vowel sound.

drew	goose	could	full
flute	good	true	should

pool	**book**
1. ____________	5. ____________
2. ____________	6. ____________
3. ____________	7. ____________
4. ____________	8. ____________

A contraction is a short way to write two words. The apostrophe takes the place of the letter ***o*** in the word ***not***.

B. Write the contraction for each pair of words.

9. should not ____________ **10.** has not ____________

11. would not ____________ **12.** could not ____________

Name ____

Read the passage. Use the summarize strategy to tell the important events in your own words.

Dr. Elizabeth Blackwell

00 Today many women are **doctors**, but that was
08 not always true. Many years ago, only men could be
18 doctors. Elizabeth Blackwell changed that.

23 **Early Life**

25 Elizabeth Blackwell was born in England in 1821. Her
34 family moved to America when Elizabeth was eleven.
42 When she got older, she became a teacher. In that time,
53 teaching was a common occupation, or job, for women.

62 **Becoming a Doctor**

65 Then one of Elizabeth's friends got very ill. She wanted
75 sick people to have less pain and discomfort. Elizabeth
84 started thinking about ways to help people like her
93 friend. She wanted to become a doctor.

Name ______________________________

100 Elizabeth talked to men doctors who told her that
109 women could not go to **medical school**. Elizabeth did not
119 agree or accept that. She tried to get into a number of
131 medical schools. She did not give up.

138 At last, she was allowed to study at a school in New
150 York. Elizabeth studied and learned medicine for two
158 years. In 1849, she became the first woman doctor in
168 America.

169 A few years later, Elizabeth opened her own medical
178 office in New York City. She asked two other women
188 doctors to join her **practice**. One of these doctors was
198 her sister, Emily. The doctors took care of sick women
208 and children. They also ran a school to train, or teach,
219 other women as doctors.

223 Elizabeth Blackwell helped people her whole life. She
231 opened the door for women doctors.

Name ______________________________

A. Reread the passage and answer the questions.

1. What happened first in Elizabeth Blackwell's life?

____

____

2. What happened next?

____

____

3. What happened last?

____

____

B. Work with a partner. Read the passage aloud. Pay attention to how you pause and group words together. Stop after one minute. Fill out the chart.

	Words Read	–	Number of Errors	=	Words Correct Score
First Read		–		=	
Second Read		–		=	

Name ______________________________

Read the selection. Complete the Sequence chart.

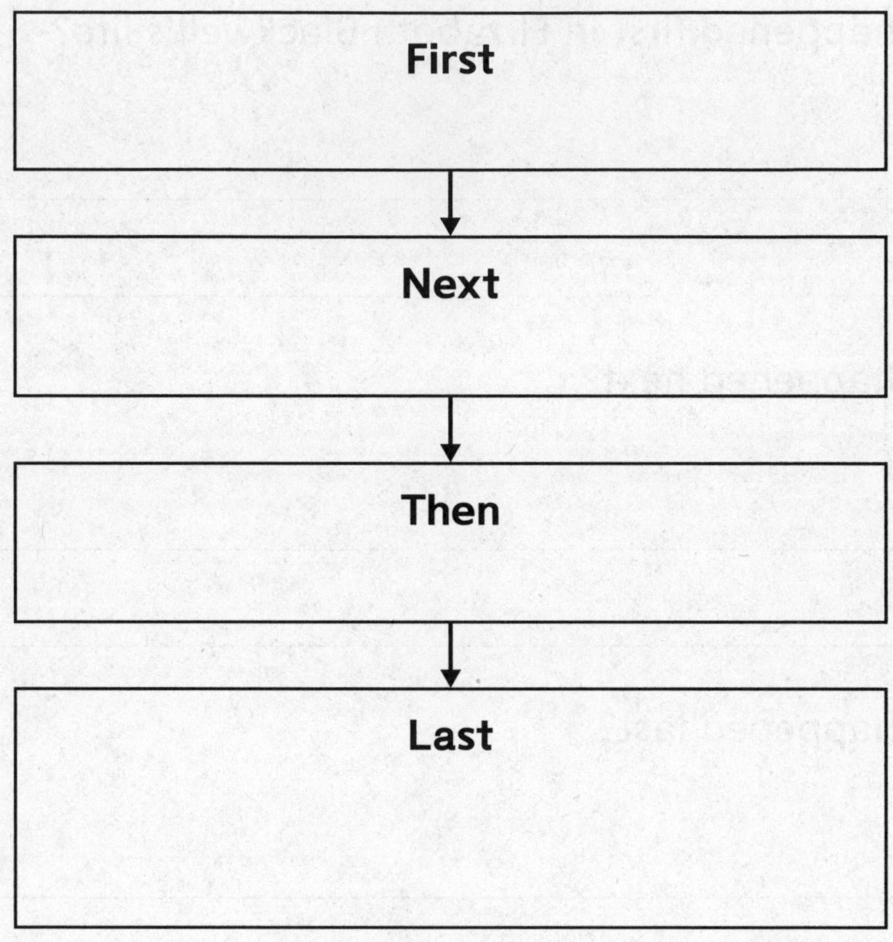

Name ______________________________

Jesse Owens

In junior high school, Jesse Owens joined the track team. He set **records** in running. Later, at age 22, Jesse won races in the **Olympics**. He proved that everyone can do great things.

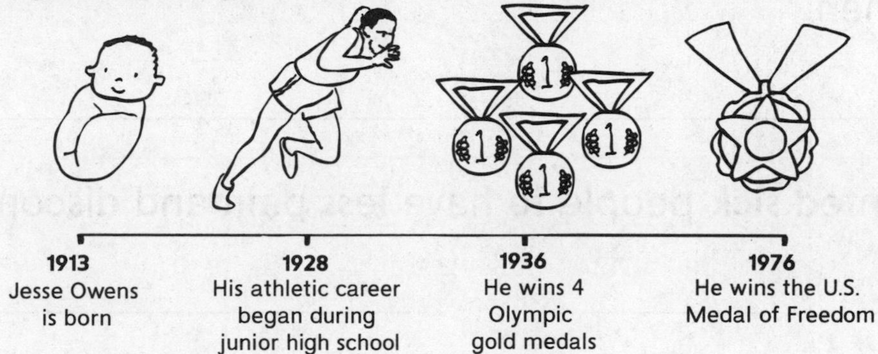

Answer the questions about the text.

1. How do you know this is a biography?

____

2. Why are the words **records** and **Olympics** in bold print?

____

3. What information does the time line help you learn?

____

4. What happened to Jesse Owens in 1936?

____

Name ______________________________

Synonyms are words that have almost the same meaning.

Read each sentence. Write the two words that are synonyms.

1. In that time, teaching was a common occupation, or job, for women.

_______________ _______________

2. She wanted sick people to have less pain and discomfort.

_______________ _______________

3. Elizabeth did not agree or accept that.

_______________ _______________

4. Elizabeth studied and learned medicine for two years.

_______________ _______________

5. They also ran a school to train, or teach, other women as doctors.

_______________ _______________

Name ______________________________

A. Read the draft model. Use the questions that follow the draft to help you think about the correct sequence of events.

Draft Model

Doug grew up in the city. When Doug got older, he helped out at the library. Today, he helps students with their reading. He liked to read when he was a boy.

1. What happens first in Doug's life?
2. What happens next?
3. What does Doug do today?

B. Now revise the draft by including events in the correct sequence in which they happened in Doug's life.

____

____

____

____

____

____

____

Name ____

Ahmed used text evidence to answer the prompt: *How are Bessie Coleman and Kate Shelley both heroes?*

Bessie Coleman and Kate Shelley are both heroes because they changed people's lives.

Bessie Coleman was determined to learn to fly, but she faced many challenges. Not many women became pilots in the early 1900s. She worked in Chicago and saved her money. Then she traveled to France to learn to fly in 1920. On June 15, 1921, she became the first African-American woman to become a lady pilot. Her dream of opening a school to teach others to fly came true after her death. She inspired other people to fly and follow their dreams.

On July 6, 1881, Kate Shelley stopped a train in the middle of the night. She crawled in the middle of the night to warn a station master that a bridge was out. If the train had continued, many people would have died. She did not think of herself, but of other people.

Both women were brave and faced many challenges. They are true heroes.

Reread the passage. Follow the directions below.

1. **Circle** the sentence in which Ahmed introduces the topic.

2. **Draw a box** around the sequence, or order, in which Bessie became a pilot.

3. **Underline** a detail about the challenges that Kate faced.

4. **Write** a possessive pronoun that Ahmed used.

____

Name ____

curious	distance	Earth resources	enormous
gently	proudly	rarely	supply

Read the story. Choose words from the box to complete the sentences. Then write the answers on the lines.

Sam was eager to learn, or ______________ about coal. He traveled quite a ______________ to the library. There he found an ______________ book. It was about ______________. The book was ______________ used, so it looked new. Sam did not want to rip the pages, so he turned them ______________. He learned that there is a ______________ of coal underground. Sam ______________ reported all he had learned about coal to his class.

Name ______________________________

The letters ***a, aw, au, augh, al,*** and ***ough*** can stand for the vowel sound you hear in ***call, dawn, sauce, caught, salt,*** and ***thought***.

A. Read each word. Circle the word that has the same vowel sound as the first word. Write it on the line. Underline the letters that spell the vowel sound.

1. **yawn** bank fault ____________
2. **cause** hawk rail ____________
3. **hall** fought last ____________
4. **walk** sale tall ____________
5. **taught** day chalk ____________

In a long word, the letters that make up a vowel team stay together in the same syllable.

B. Draw a line to divide each word into syllables. Circle the vowel team.

6. yellow
7. awful
8. pointer
9. caution

Name ____________________

Read the passage. Use the make predictions strategy to tell what you think might happen next.

The Recycling Contest

00 Ms. Hines was the principal at Grover School. Each
09 day, she saw that students threw away sheets and sheets
19 of paper. She called a meeting to talk about recycling.

29 Ms. Hines explained why recycling was important.
36 She ended her speech this way, "Let's help save the
46 Earth. If we all pitch in, we can make a difference."

57 The students cheered and went back to their rooms.
66 The next few days, Ms. Hines watched the students.
75 They were not recycling! Ms. Hines decided to try
84 another plan.

86 "Grover School is having a contest," she told the
95 students. "The class that recycles the most paper in one
105 week will win a prize. The contest begins tomorrow."

114 "Our class can win," said Eric. He was in second
124 grade.

125 His teacher, Mrs. Park, said, "Let's try our best."

Name ______________________________

134 Ms. Hines gave each class a recycling bin. She made a
145 big wall chart. Each time a class filled a bin with paper,
157 they emptied it into a giant container. Ms. Hines kept
167 track of the paper on her chart.

174 Eric reminded all his classmates to recycle. If he saw
184 someone throwing away some paper, Eric called, "Put
192 that paper in the bin." He never forgot to recycle.

202 At the end of the week, Ms. Hines called another
212 meeting. She held up the recycling chart. Eric's class had
222 won the contest!

225 "This is your prize," she said. "You get an extra ten
236 minutes outside at recess for one week. You can enjoy
246 the Earth that you are helping to save!"

Name ____

A. Reread the passage and answer the questions.

1. What is the problem in the passage?

____

____

2. What is one step that Ms. Hines takes to solve the problem?

____

____

3. What is the solution to the problem?

____

____

B. Work with a partner. Read the passage aloud. Pay attention to how you raise and lower your voice. Stop after one minute. Fill out the chart.

	Words Read	–	Number of Errors	=	Words Correct Score
First Read		–		=	
Second Read		–		=	

Name ____

Read the selection. Complete the Problem and Solution chart.

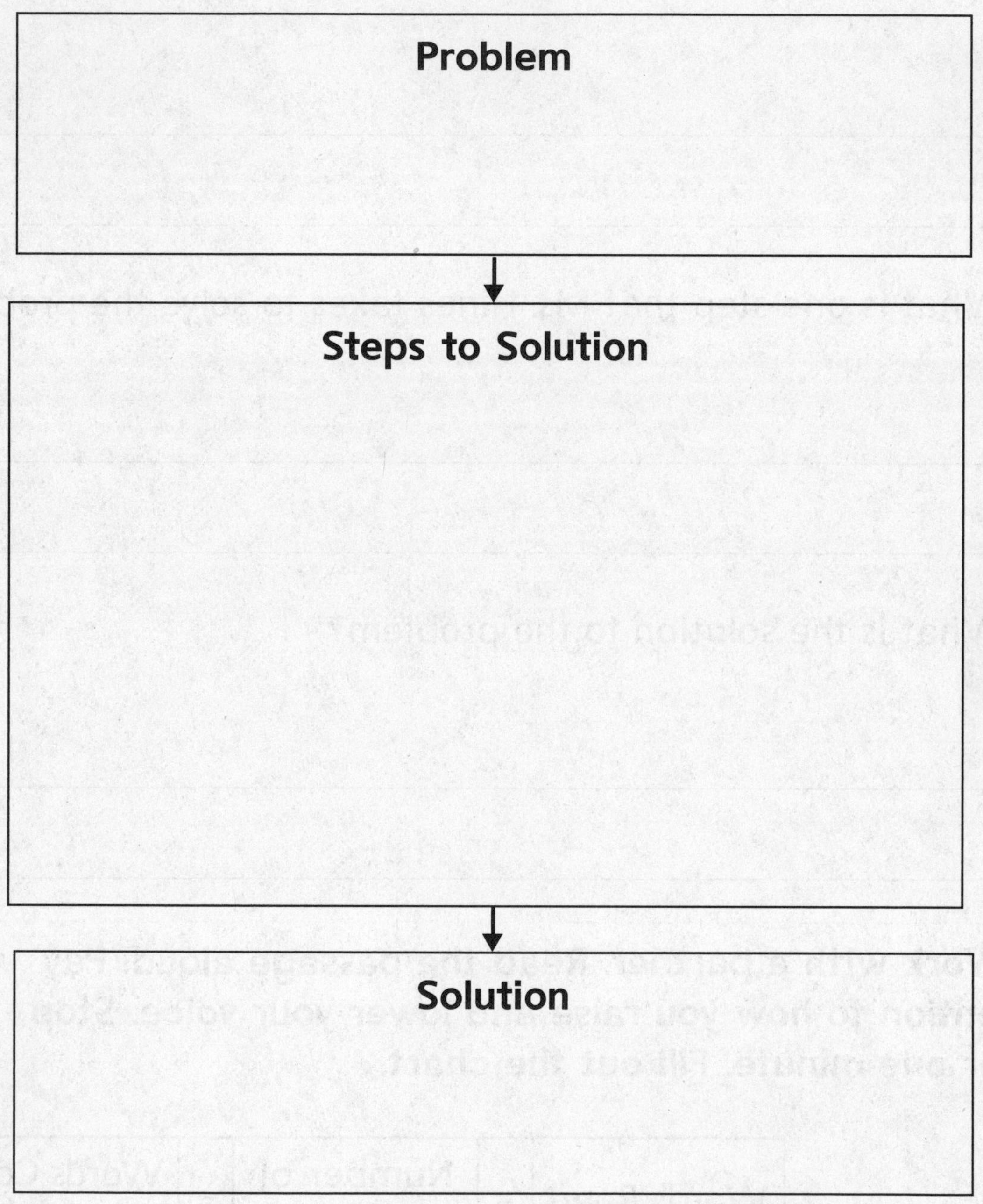

Name ______________________________

Let's Ride!

"Let's drive to the park," said Mom.

Joan said, "Driving cars can harm the Earth. Let's ride our bikes there instead."

Mom liked Joan's plan for protecting the Earth.

Answer the questions about the text.

1. How do you know this text is fiction?

____

____

2. What is Mom's dialogue in the story?

____

____

3. What is the problem?

____

4. What is the solution?

____

Name ____

Homophones are words that sound the same but have different spellings and meanings.

Read each sentence. Choose the definition that fits the homophone in bold print. Write it on the line.

1. Each day, she saw that students **threw** away sheets and sheets of paper.

   went from one side to another   tossed

   ____

2. The students cheered and went back **to** their rooms.

   in the direction of   the number after one

   ____

3. The class that recycles the most paper in one **week** will win a prize.

   seven days   not strong

   ____

4. She **made** a big wall chart.

   helper   created

   ____

Name ______________________________

A. Read the draft model. Use the questions that follow the draft to help you add linking words to connect ideas.

Draft Model

My family I went to the park for a picnic. We sat in one area. We were not happy. People had left a lot of trash there. We moved to another area. We were happy.

1. Why does the family move from the first area?
2. Why is the family happy with the second area?
3. What are some words you can use to show how ideas are connected?

B. Now revise the draft by adding words that connect ideas and help readers understand why things happen.

____

____

____

____

____

____

____

Name ______________________________

Hannah used text evidence to answer the prompt: *Add a scene to* The Woodcutter's Gift *where the community needs to decide whether to fix the town's community center or to build a new one.*

"This community center is falling apart," said the house painter. "We need a new one."

"Yes," agreed the gardener. "Let's tear it down and build a new, beautiful center for our community."

"Wait!" said Marta, a little girl who was playing with her friends on the zoo in the town center near where the men were talking. "Don't you remember what Tomás told us about the mesquite tree? He reminded us that the beauty of the tree wasn't on the outside, but it was on the inside."

"Yeah," said her friend Julio. "We need to reuse the things we have so we can protect our resources for the future."

"She's right," said the painter. "We should work together to fix up the building."

All at once, they said, "Let's get started

Reread the scene. Follow the directions below.

1. **Circle** a detail from *The Woodcutter's Gift* that tells you where the scene takes place.

2. **Draw a box** around a linking word.

3. **Underline** the text evidence that tells why reusing things is a good idea.

4. **Write** a contraction Hannah used on the line.

____

Name ____________________

exclaimed	finally	form	history
public	rules	united	writers

Read the story. Choose words from the box to complete the sentences. Then write the answers on the lines.

Throughout its long ______________, Mr. Finch's town had never had a library. He wanted everyone to be able to read books by great ______________. Mr. Finch ______________, "We need a ______________ library that everyone can use!"

Mr. Finch followed the town's strict ______________. He took his time to make, or ______________, a group. The people in the group were joined, or ______________, in their cause. After much work, Mr. Finch and his group ______________ got a library built for their town!

Name ____

The letters ***ea*** can stand for the vowel sound you hear in ***bread***.
The letters ***ou*** can stand for the vowel sound you hear in ***touch***.
The letter ***y*** can stand for the vowel sound you hear in ***myth***.

A. Read each word. Circle the word that has the same vowel sound as the first word. Write it on the line. Underline the letters that spell the vowel sound.

1. **rough** double count ______________
2. **thread** steak wealth ______________
3. **myth** find gym ______________
4. **head** breath please ______________

When two words begin with the same letter, you can look at the second letter to put the word in alphabetical order.

B. Read the words in each row. Write them in alphabetical order.

5. after, apple, ahead ______________________________
6. couple, class, crumb ______________________________
7. swim, saddle, south ______________________________
8. lead, lucky, land ______________________________

Name ______________________________

Read the passage. Use the make predictions strategy to tell what you think you might read about.

Sports Rules

Rules are important in sports. Rules tell players how
09 to play a game. They tell how to score points. They tell
21 how a game is won. They also tell players what they
32 can and cannot do. All players in a game must agree to
44 the same rules. Sometimes a player breaks a rule. Then
54 he or she may not be allowed to play for all or part of
68 the game.

70 **Basketball Rules**

72 Have you ever played basketball? If not, the name
81 "basketball" gives you a clue about some of the rules.
91 Basketball is played with a ball on a basketball court.
101 Players score points by throwing the ball through a
110 basket, or hoop.

113 There are rules about how to move the ball in
123 basketball. Players must dribble, or bounce, the ball.
131 They may also pass, or throw, the ball to another player.
142 They may not hold the ball and run with it. This would
154 not allow other players a chance to get the ball.

Name ______________________________

Sport	Number of Players	Moving the Ball	Scoring
baseball	9	throw and hit	cross home plate for one run
basketball	5	dribble and pass	shoot basket for points

164 **Baseball Rules**

166 Baseball rules are different from basketball rules. The
174 pitcher from one team throws a ball to the batter on the
186 other team. The batter gets three chances to hit the ball
197 with a bat. Sometimes the batter misses. This is called
207 a strike. After three strikes, the batter is out. Then it is
219 another batter's turn.

222 When the batter hits the ball, he or she runs around
233 four bases. The last base is home plate. The batter
243 crosses home plate to score a run. The other team tries
254 to get the batter out. They can tag the batter with the
266 ball. Then the batter cannot score a run.

274 Without rules, sports would be confusing. No one
282 would know the way to play a game. Rules make every
293 player a good sport!

Name ______________________________

A. Reread the passage and answer the questions.

1. Why are rules important in sports?

____

____

2. What happens when a basketball player shoots the ball through the hoop?

____

____

3. What happens when a batter in baseball gets three strikes?

____

____

B. Work with a partner. Read the passage aloud. Pay attention to pronunciation. Stop after one minute. Fill out the chart.

	Words Read	–	Number of Errors	=	Words Correct Score
First Read		–		=	
Second Read		–		=	

Name ______________________________

Read the selection. Complete the Cause and Effect chart.

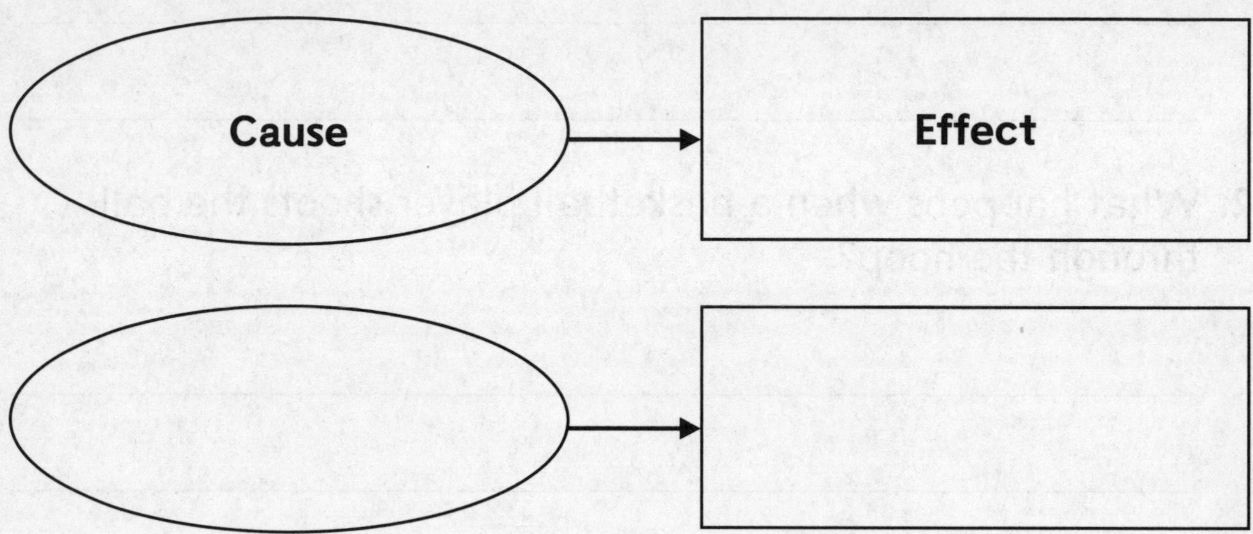

Name ______________________________

Safety Rules

Here are some ways to stay safe while having fun. When you ride a bike, wear a helmet. Wear a helmet and pads when you skateboard. If you take a trip in the car, always wear a seat belt.

Activity	Safety Equipment
bike ride	
skateboarding	
boat ride	
car ride	

Answer the questions about the text.

1. How do you know this is expository text?

____

2. What information can you learn from the chart?

____

3. What should someone wear when going for a boat ride?

____

Name ______________________________

Multiple-meaning words have more than one meaning. Use other words in the sentence to figure out which meaning is being used.

Read each sentence. Choose the meaning of the word in bold print. Write it on the line.

1. **Rules** are important in sports.

   things that tell how to behave make laws and decide things

   ____

2. Rules tell players how to **play** a game.

   a story that is acted out to take part in a sports game

   ____

3. Basketball is played with a ball on a basketball **court**.

   the place where a ruler lives an area used for playing a sport

   ____

4. Players must **dribble**, or bounce, the ball.

   to move a ball by bouncing to spill drops of liquid

   ____

5. The pitcher throws a ball to the **batter** on the other team.

   a mixture used in cooking a player who hits a baseball

   ____

Name ______________________________

A. Read the draft model. Use the questions that follow the draft to help you think about how to make the writing more informal.

Draft Model

We have a great school because everyone follows the rules! Here are some of the rules. Walk in the halls. Do not run. Respect teachers and students. Enjoy learning every day.

1. Where could you use contractions?

2. Where could you add exclamations?

3. Which sentences could you change to make the writing sound more like natural speaking?

B. Now revise the draft by using a more informal voice, one that sounds like natural speaking.

____

____

____

____

____

____

Name ______________________________

Dean used text evidence to answer the prompt: *What do the symbols of our country tell about what is important to us? Use a formal voice.*

The symbols of our country tell us about what is important to us. The Liberty Bell, the Statue of Liberty, and the Constitution stand for freedom. Freedom is very important to Americans. In the selection "Setting the Rules" on page 483, the text says that the Constitution "gives rights, or privileges, to all the people." It also explains the Constitution gives Americans the right to express their ideas. On page 483, I read that Americans are even free to change their Constitution.

On page 485 of "American Symbols," I read the Statue of Liberty is a "symbol of freedom and hope." In "Setting the Rules" it says rules are added to the Constitution to help make a better life for people. The freedom to believe and to live the way you want is important to Americans. In "Visiting the Past" I read that the Liberty Bell rang for freedom when the Declaration of Independence was read for the first time. The Liberty Bell is in Philadelphia for people to visit. The symbols of America remind us about what our country stands for.

Reread the paragraphs. Follow the directions below.

1. **Circle** a word that Dean used to show formal voice.
2. **Draw** a box around a detail Dean included from "American Symbols."
3. **Underline** Dean's concluding sentence.
4. **Write** an example of pronoun-verb agreement on the line.

____

Name ____

appeared	crops	develop	edge
golden	rustled	shining	stages

Read the story. Choose words from the box to complete the sentences. Then write the answers on the lines.

The farmer had tried growing different _______________, but each one failed. "I must _______________ new seeds," thought the farmer. So this is what he did. He planted different kinds of seeds and recorded their _______________ of growth.

Then the farmer chose the best seeds and planted them in his fields. Soon green sprouts _______________. After many weeks, the farmer saw the _______________ wheat growing. It grew fast in the _______________ sun. The wheat _______________ in the wind. The farmer walked along the _______________ of his fields, proud of what he had done.

Name ______________________________

A syllable must always have a vowel. When a syllable ends in a vowel, it is an **open syllable** and usually has a long vowel sound, as in ***frozen, fro / zen***. When a syllable ends in a consonant, it is a **closed syllable** and usually has a short vowel sound, as in ***kitten, kit / ten***.

A. Draw a line between the syllables in each word. Then write each syllable.

1. magnet ____________ ____________

2. robot ____________ ____________

3. hidden ____________ ____________

4. pencil ____________ ____________

5. crayon ____________ ____________

A **compound word** is a word that is made up of two smaller words.

B. Read each sentence. Circle the compound word. Write its meaning.

6. The student wrote in his notebook. ____________

7. The girl painted her bedroom. ____________

8. Plants need water and sunlight. ____________

Name ____

Read the passage. Use the reread strategy to check your understanding of story events.

The Contest of Athens

Long ago, the city of Athens needed a patron,
9 someone to watch over the city. There were two great
19 beings who wished to be the patron. One was Poseidon,
29 who ruled the seas. The other was Athena, who had
39 great wisdom.

41 The king of Athens had to select one of these two. So
53 he asked each one to give a valuable and important gift
64 to Athens.

66 "Your gift must be something useful for the city," said
76 the king.

78 It was Poseidon's turn first. He hit the ground with his
89 spear, the long-handled blade he always carried. From
98 the ground, a well appeared. Water began to flow.

107 The king hurried to the well to taste the water. He
118 found that the water was as salty as the sea.

128 "This will not do as a gift to Athens," he said.

Name ______________________________

139 Next, it was Athena's turn. She also hit the ground
149 with her spear. In that spot, she buried an olive branch
160 in the ground to make an olive tree. The olive tree
171 would give the people of Athens food, oil, and wood.

181 The king was very happy with Athena's fine gift. He
191 stated, "Because you have given us this olive tree, I will
202 make you the patron of Athens."

208 Athena was pleased, but Poseidon was dejected at
216 losing the contest. He flooded the land with seawater.
225 Once he calmed down, he drained the floodwater away.

Name ______________________________

A. Reread the passage and answer the questions.

1. What was Poseidon's gift to Athens? How did the king feel about Poseidon's gift?

____

____

2. What was Athena's gift to Athens? How did the king feel about Athena's gift?

____

____

3. What is the theme of the passage?

____

____

B. Work with a partner. Read the passage aloud. Pay attention to how you use your voice to show feelings. Stop after one minute. Fill out the chart.

	Words Read	–	Number of Errors	=	Words Correct Score
First Read		–		=	
Second Read		–		=	

Name ______________________________

Read the selection. Complete the Theme chart.

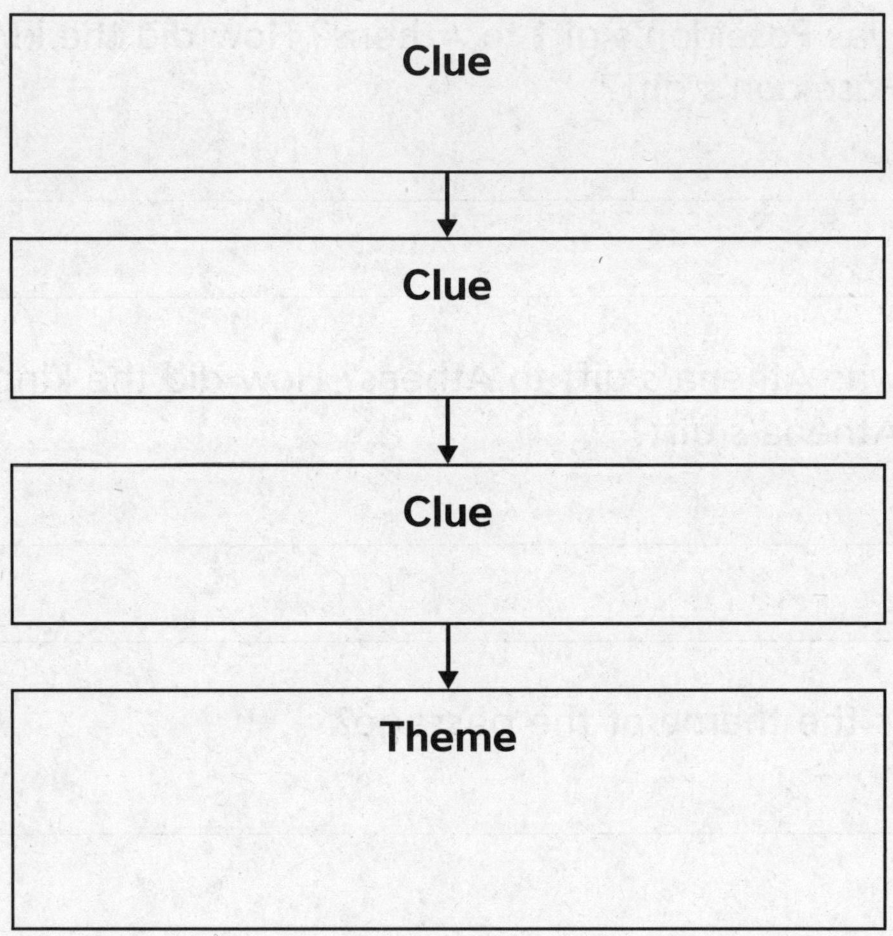

Name ______________________________

Clytie and Apollo

Apollo was the ruler of the sun. Clytie loved to watch Apollo as he moved across the sky. She watched him so often that she became a sunflower. Even today sunflowers turn to the sun.

Answer the questions about the text.

1. How do you know that this text is a myth?

____

____

2. Who is Apollo?

____

3. Why does Clytie look up at the sky?

____

4. What does the myth explain?

____

____

Name ____

Look at this example of **context clues** in a sentence. The underlined words help explain what *select* means.

The king of Athens had to **select** one of these two.

Read each sentence. Write the meaning of the word in bold print. Underline the context clues in the sentence that helped you.

1. Long ago, the city of Athens needed a **patron**, someone to watch over the city.

____

2. So he asked each one to give a **valuable** and important gift to Athens.

____

3. He hit the ground with his **spear**, the long-handled blade he always carried.

____

4. In that spot, she **buried** an olive branch in the ground to make an olive tree.

____

5. Athena was pleased, but Poseidon was **dejected** at losing the contest.

____

Name ____

A. Read the draft model. Use the questions that follow the draft to help you think about a strong opening you can add.

Draft Model

Once there was a flower. It was in a forest. It needed rain.

1. What does the flower look like? How does it feel and act?

2. What does the forest look like?

3. What problem might the flower have?

B. Now revise the draft by writing a strong opening that tells about the character, the setting, and a problem.

____

____

____

____

____

____

____

____

____

Name ____

Andre used text evidence to answer the prompt: *Would you prefer to have a seed for the pumpkin in* The Golden Flower *or a seed for the pumpkin in "A Pumpkin Plant"?*

I would prefer to have a seed for the kind of pumpkin described in "A Pumpkin Plant." The pumpkin in *A Golden Flower* shines like the sun, but there are no seeds inside. It is filled with water and sea creatures. I would like to have a pumpkin that has seeds inside it so that I can grow more pumpkins. I would plant the seeds in my garden. My garden is in a sunny spot in the backyard. The pumpkin plant's flowers would make my garden really colorful!

In the fall, I would decorate some of the pumpkins and leave them outside for everybody to see. Then, I would take some seeds from inside those pumpkins and plant them in my garden, too. This is why I prefer to have a seed from the kind of pumpkin in "A Pumpkin Plant."

Reread the paragraphs. Follow the directions below.

1. **Circle** the sentence where Andre states his opinion.

2. **Draw a box** around two linking words.

3. **Underline** text evidence Andre included about why his garden would be a good place for a pumpkin seed.

4. **Write** an adjective that tells "what kind" on the line.

____

Name ______________________________

electricity	energy	flows	haul
power	silent	solar	underground

Use what you know about the words in the sentences to choose the word that makes sense in each blank. Then write the word on the line.

1. Will you help me ______________ these bags of leaves to the shed?

2. We can get ______________ from eating healthful foods.

3. The classroom was ______________ during the test.

4. Moving water has the ______________ to move rocks.

5. Worms make their home ______________.

6. A river ______________ through the middle of the city.

7. The man set up a ______________ panel on the roof of his house to collect the sun's rays.

8. We cannot turn on a light without ______________.

Name ______________________________

A syllable that has the **vowel consonant e** pattern often has the long vowel sound. In the word *excite,* the syllable *cite* has the long *i* sound.

A. Circle four words in the box that have a vowel consonant *e* syllable. Then write the syllables in each circled word.

compete tiger replace zebra arrive pollute

1. ________ ________ **2.** ________ ________

3. ________ ________ **4.** ________ ________

A **prefix** is added to the beginning of a word. A **suffix** is added to the end of a word.

Prefixes	**Suffixes**
re- = "again"	***-ful*** = "full of"
un- and ***dis-*** = "not" or "opposite of"	***-less*** = "without"

B. Read each clue. Write a word with a prefix or a suffix to match each clue.

5. full of joy ____________ **6.** not wise ____________

7. without fear ____________ **8.** visit again ____________

9. the opposite of approve ____________

Name ____

Read the passage. Use the reread strategy to check your understanding of new information or difficult facts.

Ocean Energy

We use energy every day to do work. With energy, we
11 can turn on a light, heat a home, cook food, and run a
24 computer. Much of our energy comes from coal, oil, and
34 gas. Some of our energy comes from the sun and the
45 wind. One day, we might even get our energy from the
56 ocean.

57 Yes, energy can come from the ocean. There are not
67 many ocean power plants right now. But the ocean is a
78 big source of energy.

82 **Tidal Energy**

84 The ocean has high and low tides. This means the
94 water rises and falls every twelve hours. This tidal
103 energy can be used to make power.

110 When high tide flows in to shore, the water is trapped
121 behind a dam. The water is stored in a large pool. When
133 low tide occurs, the water behind the dam is let out.
144 The rushing water runs a machine inside the dam. The
154 machine makes electricity.

Name ______________________________

157 **Ocean Wave Energy**

160 The water in the ocean is always moving. The
169 movement of ocean waves can run a machine built to
179 produce power. The waves move up and down inside the
189 machine. They spin parts of the machine. The machine
198 makes electricity.

200 **Heat Energy**

202 The water temperature on the ocean's surface is
210 warmer than below. That's because the sun heats the
219 water on top. Deep below the surface, the water is very
230 cold.

231 This temperature difference creates heat energy. A
238 power plant uses this heat energy to make electricity.

247 The ocean is a giant source of energy. Maybe one day
258 the ocean will power the world.

Name ____

A. Reread the passage and answer the questions.

1. What is this passage about?

____

____

2. What is one fact that the author includes about ocean energy?

____

____

3. What is another fact that the author includes about ocean energy?

____

____

4. What is the author's purpose for writing this passage?

____

B. Work with a partner. Read the passage aloud. Pay attention to how you use intonation. Stop after one minute. Fill out the chart.

	Words Read	–	Number of Errors	=	Words Correct Score
First Read		–		=	
Second Read		–		=	

Name ____

Read the selection. Complete the Author's Purpose chart.

Clue	**Clue**

Author's Purpose

Name ______________________________

Each Can Counts

Recycling a can means that the same material can be used again. Energy is not wasted getting new materials to make a new can. The energy saved by recycling one can may run a TV for three hours.

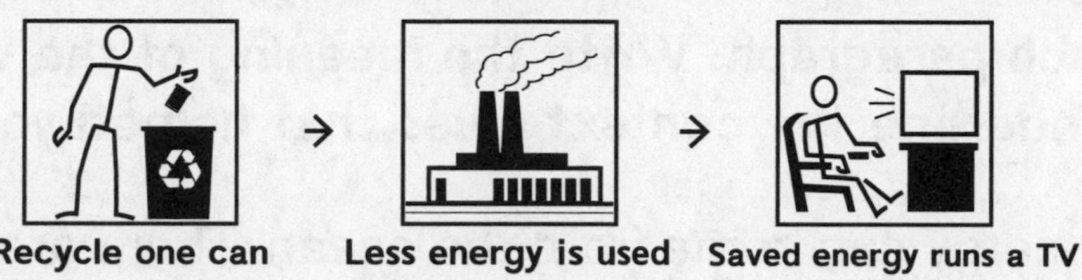

Answer the questions about the text.

1. How do you know this is expository text?

____

____

2. Why is it important to recycle cans?

____

3. What information does the diagram show?

____

____

4. What action does the first label tell about?

____

____

Name ______________________________

Look at this example of **context clues** in a paragraph. The underlined words help explain what *energy* means.

We use **energy** every day to do work. With energy, we can turn on a light, heat a home, cook food, and run a computer.

Read each paragraph. Write the meaning of the word in bold print. Underline the context clues that helped you.

1. Yes, energy can come from the ocean. There are not many ocean power plants right now. But the ocean is a big **source** of energy.

____

2. The ocean has high and low **tides**. This means the water rises and falls every twelve hours. This tidal energy can be used to make power.

____

3. The movement of ocean waves can run a machine built to produce power. The waves move up and down inside the machine. They spin parts of the machine. The machine makes **electricity**.

____

4. The water temperature on the ocean's **surface** is warmer than below. That's because the sun heats the water on top. Deep below the surface, the water is very cold.

____

Name ______________________________

A. Read the draft model. Use the questions that follow the draft to help you think about adding content words.

Draft Model

A radio needs something to make it work. It can run on electricity. It can also run on a battery. Some radios have a sun panel to charge the battery.

1. What content words can you add to tell about a radio?

2. What content words can you add to tell about electricity?

3. What content words can you add to tell about a battery?

B. Now revise the draft by adding content words that are related to radios, electricity, and batteries.

____

____

____

____

____

____

____

Name ____

Héctor used text evidence to answer the prompt: *How do people depend on Earth for energy?*

People depend on the sunlight and the water on Earth for energy. The Sun's energy goes into the water on Earth. People trap the energy in dams and use it to make electricity. The electricity travels through power lines to help light our towns and cities. Water is recycled in the water cycle. It never disappears, so it is always there to use. People also depend on Earth for water to drink. And the Sun gives us food to eat. Plants use the Sun's energy to grow. We eat the plants then the energy is in us! People depend on Earth to give us electricity, water to drink, and food to eat.

Reread the passage. Follow the directions below.

1. **Circle** one fact Héctor used from "The Power of Water."
2. **Draw a box** around one content word that Héctor used.
3. **Underline** a detail Héctor used to develop his point.
4. **Write** the article that appears twice in the first sentence on the line.

____

Name ______________________________

exploration	important	machines	prepare
repair	result	scientific	teamwork

Choose the word that makes sense in each blank. Then write the word on the line.

1. Lawn mowers are ______________ that make it easier to cut grass.
2. She will study the honeybees in a ______________ way.
3. I need to ______________ this broken computer.
4. It's ______________ to listen when someone speaks to you.
5. The scientists planned for a rain forest ______________.
6. The ______________ of the heavy rain was a flood.
7. How will you ______________ for your camping trip?
8. Use ______________ to do a job that is too big for one person.

Name ____

When a word ends in a consonant plus ***-le, -el,*** or ***-al,*** the consonant and the letters *-le, -el,* or *-al* often make the last syllable in the word, as in ***needle, bagel,*** and ***local***.

A. Draw a line between the syllables in each word. Then write each syllable.

1. hazel ____________ ____________
2. purple ____________ ____________
3. sandal ____________ ____________
4. cable ____________ ____________

A **contraction** is used to combine two words. An apostrophe takes the place of a missing letter or letters: ***do not = don't***.

A **possessive noun** has an apostrophe and the letter *s* to show ownership: ***Mom's car***.

B. Read each sentence. Look at the underlined word. If it is a contraction, write the two words. If it is a possessive noun, write to tell who or what owns or has what.

5. The boy <u>couldn't</u> get his toy robot to work.

____

6. The <u>boy's</u> father put in a new battery.

____

Name ______________________________

Read the passage. Use the summarize strategy to tell the important ideas in your own words.

An Antarctic Team

Teams of people explore places all over the globe.
09 Why do they work in teams? Each person has special
19 skills that help out the whole team.
26

The Antarctic is an incredible place to explore. Each
35 year, teams travel there to study the region. Each team
45 member has an important job to do.
52

One of the first jobs is to set up a research station,
65 or base camp. This is where people live and work and
76 set off on field trips. Some team members construct the
85 camp's buildings.
87

People can reach the camp by air. Pilots fly planes
97 and helicopters. They transport people and equipment
104 to the camp.

Name ______________________________

A plane flies team members home from the camp.

107 Scientists work as part of the team to learn more
117 about the Antarctic. Each scientist conducts a different
125 project. Some study the animal and plant life. Some
134 study the climate and weather. Some study the glaciers.

143 Other team members take care of buildings and
151 vehicles. Some people inspect the camp's electricity
158 system to make sure it is working. Some people fix
168 broken equipment.

170 A doctor and a nurse take care of sick team members.
181 There are firefighters who work to prevent fires.

189 Exploring the Antarctic is not a job for one person.
199 A whole team must be involved. And each team
208 member must do the job he or she knows best.

Name ______________________________

A. Reread the passage and answer the questions.

1. What was one key detail from the passage?

____

____

2. What was another key detail from the passage?

____

____

3. What is the main idea of the passage?

____

____

B. Work with a partner. Read the passage aloud. Pay attention to how you pronounce the words. Stop after one minute. Fill out the chart.

	Words Read	–	Number of Errors	=	Words Correct Score
First Read		–		=	
Second Read		–		=	

Name ______________________________

Read the selection. Complete the Main Idea and Key Details chart.

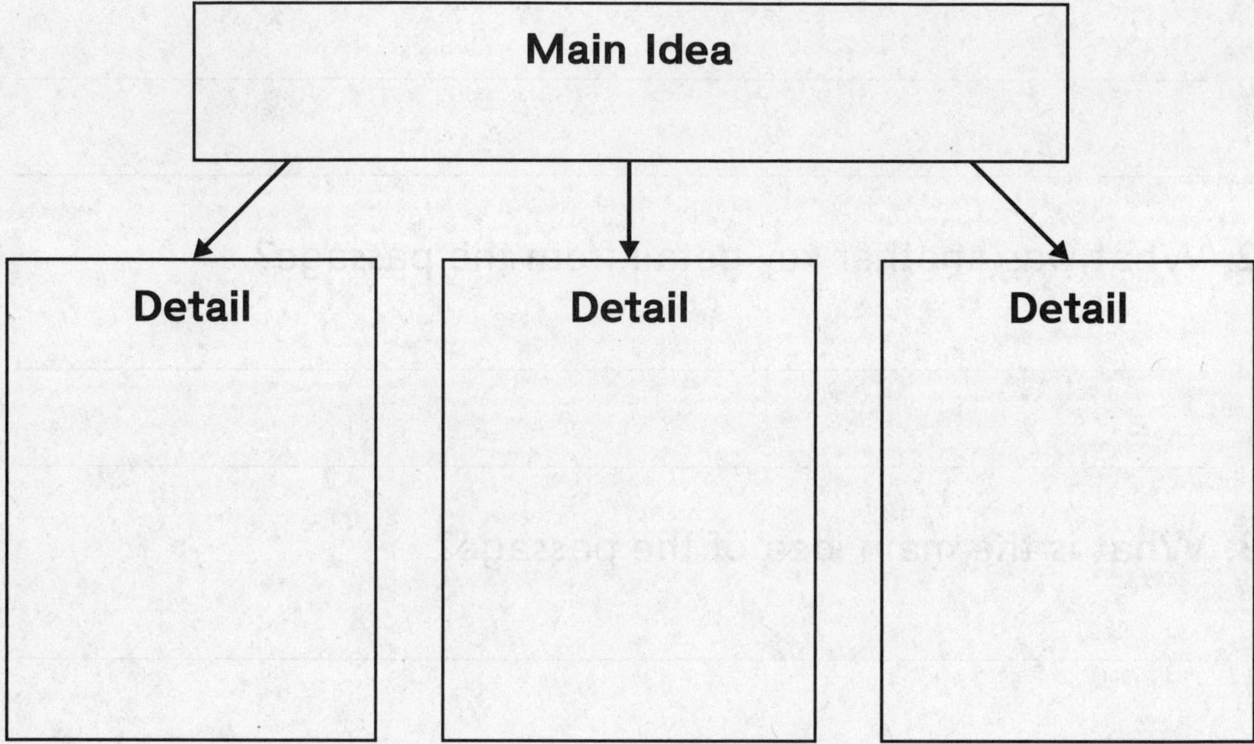

Name ______________________________

A Baby Mammoth

A reindeer herder in Russia found a baby mammoth's body. She was moved to a museum. Scientists from around the world studied the baby. She was sent to Japan for tests. Scientists tried to learn all they could.

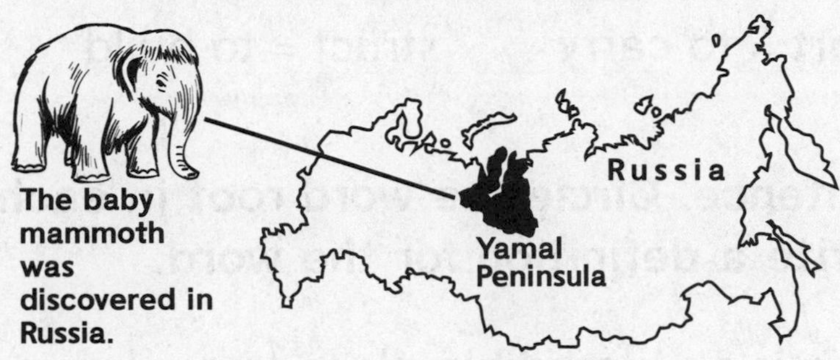

The baby mammoth was discovered in Russia.

Answer the questions about the text.

1. How do you know this is expository text?

____

____

2. How did people work as a team when the baby mammoth was discovered?

____

____

3. What information can you learn from the map?

____

____

Name ______________________________

You can figure out the meaning of unfamiliar words by looking for **word roots**. Some English words have Greek or Latin roots.

cred = to believe	spect = to look
duc = to lead	sta = to stand
port = to carry	struct = to build

Read each sentence. Circle the word root in each bold print word. Then write a definition for the word.

1. The Antarctic is an **incredible** place to explore.

____

2. One of the first jobs is to set up a research **station**, or base camp.

____

3. Some team members **construct** the camp's buildings.

____

4. They **transport** people and equipment to the camp.

____

5. Some people **inspect** the camp's electricity system to make sure it is working.

____

Name ______________________________

A. Read the draft model. Use the questions that follow the draft to help you think about details you can add to support the main idea.

Draft Model

Teamwork is important for jungle explorers. There are many different jobs for team members. One team member reads maps so that the other team members know where they are.

1. Why does the team need maps?

2. What other kinds of jobs might team members have?

3. What other details can you add to show why teamwork is important?

B. Now revise the draft by adding details that support and explain the main idea of teamwork.

____

____

____

____

____

____

Name ____________________

Melissa used text evidence to answer the prompt: *Would you rather be an astronaut or a mountain climber?*

I would rather be an astronaut than a mountain climber. They both seem like hard work, but I think being an astronaut looks more exciting. I read that different kinds of people can become astronauts. I could become an astronaut, too! I would learn how to fly so that I can be the pilot of the space shuttle. I would get to wear a space suit with a TV camera in it, but I think I would have to wait until I'm older. The space suit is heavier than I am. It weighs 280 pounds! I could also float in a special plane called the Vomit Comet. I hope I don't get sick. To be a mountain climber, you have to do a lot of exercise to prepare. Team Jordan ran long distances carrying heavy backpacks and pulling tires. When they were near the top of the mountain, they had to wear oxygen masks so that they didn't get sick. I would rather float in space than have to pull tires!

Reread the passage. Follow the directions below.

1. **Circle** the sentence that tells the topic of the paragraph.

2. **Draw a box** around a supporting detail about why Melissa will have to wait to be an astronaut.

3. **Underline** Melissa's strong conclusion.

4. **Write** on the line an adjective that compares.

____

Name ______________________________

invented	money	prices	purchase
record	system	value	worth

A. Choose the word that makes sense for each clue. Write the word on the line.

1. how much something is worth ______________
2. facts that are written down about something ______________
3. made something that was not around before ______________
4. how much you have to pay to buy things ______________
5. a plan or set of rules for doing something ______________
6. the value of something ______________
7. the dollars and cents you can use to buy things ______________
8. to get something by paying money ______________

B. Choose one vocabulary word from the box above. Write the word in a sentence of your own.

9. ____

____

____

Name ______________________________

Vowel teams such as ***ai, ay, oa, ow, oi, oy, oo,*** and ***ew*** can help you read longer words with more than one syllable.

A. Read each word. Write the word from the box that has the same vowel team. Circle the letters in the vowel team.

raisin	vowel	soapy	cocoon

1. toaster ______________ **2. powder** ______________

3. sooner ______________ **4. contain** ______________

The ending *-er* is added to an adjective to compare two nouns. The ending *-est* is added to an adjective to compare more than two nouns. Make these spelling changes before adding an ending:

- words ending in *y*: change *y* to *i*
- words with final *e*: drop the final *e*
- words ending with a vowel and a consonant: double the final consonant

B. Add *-er* and *-est* to each word. Write the new words.

1. big ______________ ______________

2. slim ______________ ______________

3. windy ______________ ______________

Name ______________________________

Read the passage. Use the summarize strategy to tell the important ideas in your own words.

Make a Budget

You get some money, but you spend it all and have
11 nothing left. What can you do to take control? You can
22 make a budget to manage your money.

29 What Is a Budget?

33 A budget is a plan to keep track of money coming in
45 and money going out. The government has a budget.
54 Many families have a budget. You can have a budget,
64 too.

65 Income

66 First, think about money you get. Where does the
75 money come from? You might get an allowance, you
84 might earn money from a job, or you might get money
95 as a gift. All the money you get is called income.

106 Expenses

107 Now think about money you need to spend. Where
116 does the money go? You might have to buy lunch or pay
128 for music class. The money you spend is called expenses.

Name ____

138 Spending Money

140 Subtract the expenses from the income. The amount
148 that is left is money you can spend on things you want.
160 You may not have enough money to buy an item you
171 want, though.

173 Here's what you can do. Set a savings goal for the
184 item. Each time you get money, set aside a portion, or
195 part, of it. You might have to save for a few weeks or a
209 few months, depending on the cost of your item. Keep
219 saving until you reach your goal. Then you can buy
229 your item.

231 Many people make a budget to manage their money.
240 You can make a budget to make your money work for
251 you. A budget will help you pay your expenses and
261 save money to buy things you want.

Name ____

A. Reread the passage and answer the questions.

1. What problem was described in the first paragraph of the passage?

____

____

2. What was one step to solving the problem?

____

____

3. What was the solution to the problem?

____

____

B. Work with a partner. Read the passage aloud. Pay attention to how you use intonation. Stop after one minute. Fill out the chart.

	Words Read	–	Number of Errors	=	Words Correct Score
First Read		–		=	
Second Read		–		=	

Name ______________________________

Read the selection. Complete the Problem and Solution chart.

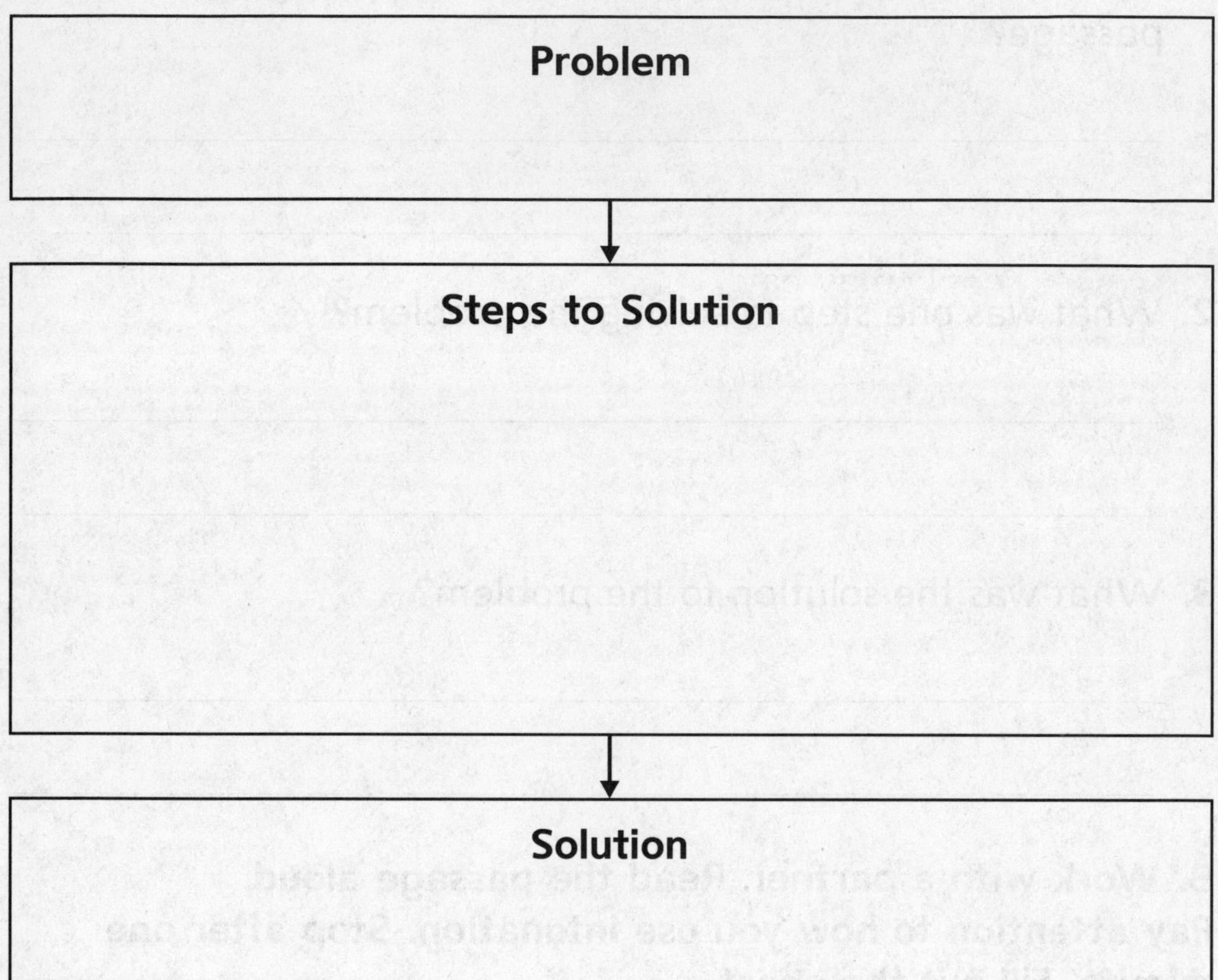

Name ______________________________

How We Pay

Money Now

To pay for things now, people use bills and coins. That may change.

Future Money

There may be no bills or coins. People may pay using only a computer or a cell phone.

Answer the questions about the text.

1. How do you know this is expository text?

____

____

2. What is the first section of text about?

____

____

3. What does the subheading tell you about the second section of text?

____

____

Name ______________________________

Look at this example of **context clues** in a paragraph. The underlined words help explain what *subtract* means.

Subtract the expenses from the income. The amount that is left is money you can spend on things you want.

Read each paragraph. Write the meaning of the word in bold print. Underline the context clues that helped you.

1. You get some money, but you spend it all and have nothing left. What can you do to take control? You can make a budget to **manage** your money.

____

2. A **budget** is a plan to keep track of money coming in and money going out. The government has a budget. Many families have a budget. You can have a budget, too.

____

3. First, think about money you get. Where does the money come from? You might get an allowance, you might earn money from a job, or you might get money as a gift. All the money you get is called **income**.

____

4. Now think about money you need to spend. Where does the money go? You might have to buy lunch or pay for music class. The money you spend is called **expenses**.

____

Name ______________________________

A. Read the draft model. Use the questions that follow the draft to help you think about a strong conclusion you can add.

Draft Model

People can save money at a bank. They can get money from the bank's ATM. People also use banks for paying their bills.

1. What is the topic of the writing?

2. What is the main idea?

3. What information could you include in a conclusion sentence?

B. Now revise the draft by writing a strong conclusion that sums up the main idea.

____

____

____

____

____

____

____

Name ____

Farah used text evidence to answer the prompt: *How do the authors of "Money Madness" and "King Midas and the Golden Touch" use sequence to organize the text?*

The authors of "Money Madness" and "King Midas and the Golden Touch" both use sequence to organize the text. They both start with the earliest event and tell the stories in the order the events happen. In "Money Madness," the author begins by describing what life was like before money existed. Then he tells all about early kinds of money, like cows and rocks. After that, he describes how the money we use today was invented.

The author of "King Midas and the Golden Touch" also uses sequence. The author uses words like "Many years ago" and "one day" to let the reader know when events took place. The author tells about King Midas's day in order. It starts in the garden during the day and ends at dinnertime. The authors of both selections used sequence to help me understand the events in the order they took place.

Reread the passage. Follow the directions below.

1. **Circle** a fact Farah included from "Money Madness."

2. **Draw a box** around two sequence words Farah used.

3. **Underline** the conclusion.

4. **Write** a prepositional phrase Farah used in the second paragraph.

____

Name ____

create	dazzling	imagination	seconds

A. Choose the word that makes sense for each clue. Write the word on the line.

1. something that is very bright ______________
2. to make or invent something ______________
3. the small parts of a minute ______________
4. the ability to form ideas in your mind ______________

B. Complete each sentence with a word from the box above.

5. How fast can you run in sixty ______________?
6. The ______________ sun was so bright it hurt my eyes.
7. Use your ______________ to write a story.
8. My sister likes to ______________ new kinds of cookies in the kitchen.

C. Choose one vocabulary word from the box above. Write the word in a sentence of your own.

9. ____

Name ______________________________

When a vowel or a pair of vowels is followed by the letter *r*, it changes the vowel sound. The vowels and the *r* stay in the same syllable.

A. Read the sentences. Circle two words in each sentence that have an *r*-controlled syllable. Write each word and divide it into syllables.

1. This morning is perfect for walking in the meadow.

____

2. The artist paints a portrait at his easel.

____

3. The farmer grows garlic to sell to people.

____

When you divide a longer word into syllables, each syllable must have a vowel sound.

B. Read each word. Draw a line between each syllable.

4. important

5. respectful

6. operator

7. afternoon

Name ______________________________

Read the poem. Use the summarize strategy to retell the poem in your own words.

Growing Up in One Day

If I could grow up in just one day,
09 how would I work to get my pay?
17 I could be a teacher
22 in a class,
25 helping children
27 to learn and pass.
31 The moving children
34 would be an army of ants,
40 walking to class in
44 a happy trance.

47 I could be a chef
52 in a busy kitchen,
56 I'd have helpers
59 that would always pitch in.
64 If a diner's stomach
68 was a bottomless pit,
72 My cook and I
76 would never sit.

Name ____

79 I could be a firefighter
84 in a truck,
87 putting out fires
90 and helping cats that are stuck.
96 My legs would be machines.
101 I'd climb so fast
105 and bring the cat down
110 safe at last.

113 I won't grow up
117 for quite awhile,
120 but I have some ideas
125 that make me smile.

Name ____

A. Reread the passage and answer the questions.

1. How does the boy feel about being a teacher when he grows up?

____

____

2. How does the boy feel about being a firefighter when he grows up?

____

____

3. What is the boy's point of view in the poem?

____

____

B. Work with a partner. Read the passage aloud. Pay attention to how you use your voice to show feelings. Stop after one minute. Fill out the chart.

	Words Read	–	Number of Errors	=	Words Correct Score
First Read		–		=	
Second Read		–		=	

Name ____

Read the selection. Complete the Point of View chart.

Character	Clue	Point of View

Name ______________________________

My Imagination

I dive with a whale deep into the sea,
I climb with a monkey up a tall tree.
I fly with an eagle and off we zoom,
I have lots of adventures
Without leaving my room.

Answer the questions about the text.

1. How do you know this text is a poem?

____

____

2. Which words at the end of lines rhyme?

____

3. What do rhyming words add to the poem?

____

____

Name ______________________________

A **metaphor** compares two different things, but it does not use the word ***like*** or ***as***.

Read the lines. Write the two things the author compares. Then explain what each metaphor means.

1. The children were an army of ants, walking to class in a happy trance.

   What two things are compared? ______________

   Both things ______________.

2. My legs were a machine, moving me to the finish line.

   What two things are compared? ______________

   Both things ______________.

3. His smile was sunlight that lit up the room.

   What two things are compared? ______________

   Both things ______________.

4. The runner was lightning in the race.

   What two things are compared? ______________

   Both things ______________.

Name ______________________________

A. Read the draft model. Use the questions that follow the draft to help you think about how to make the writing better by using strong words.

Draft Model

I paint the adventures in my mind.
I make pictures of every kind.

1. Where could you add strong adjectives?
2. Where could you add strong adverbs?
3. Which words could you replace with stronger words?

B. Now revise the draft by adding strong words.

____

____

____

____

____

____

____

Name ______________________________

Thomas used text evidence to answer the prompt: *Write a free verse or rhyming poem about how books and art let you use your imagination. Include a metaphor in the poem.*

My Moods

Whenever I am feeling blue,
Looking for something to do,
I grab paper, paints, and brush,
And quietly, without a hush
I find a corner in my room,
And plant a garden in full bloom.

No matter how I feel,
make-believe will help me heal.
It is better to let my imagination soar
Because then, my spirit will roar roar roar!

Reread the poem. Follow the directions below.

1. **Underline** the metaphor Thomas uses to describe what he paints.
2. Thomas uses strong rhyming words in his poem. Circle two rhyming words in the first stanza.
3. **Draw a box** around how Thomas chases his moods away.
4. On the line, **write** an adjective that Thomas uses.

____